Modern
PRESSURE
COOKING

Modern
PRESSURE
COOKING

More Than 100 Incredible Recipes
and Time-Saving Techniques to Master Your Pressure Cooker

BREN HERRERA

private chef and owner of BrenHerrera.com and the blog Flanboyant Eats

PAGE STREET
PUBLISHING CO.

PAGE STREET
PUBLISHING CO.

First published in 2016 by

Page Street Publishing Co.

27 Congress Street, Suite 103

Salem, MA 01970

www.pagestreetpublishing.com

Distributed by Macmillan, sales in Canada by The Canadian Manda Group.

19   18   17   16   1   2   3   4   5

ISBN-13: 978-1-62414-303-8

ISBN-10: 1-62414-303-2

Library of Congress Control Number: 2016942217

Cover and book design by Page Street Publishing Co.

Photography by Ken Goodman

Cover photo and photos on pages 73, 103, 110, 143 and 201 by Sam Brown

Styled by Bianca Borges and Bren Herrera

Printed and bound in the U.S.A.

Page Street is proud to be a member of 1% for the Planet. Members donate one percent of their sales to one or more of the over 1,500 environmental and sustainability charities across the globe who participate in this program.

*PARA TI, MAMI. MI CORAZÓN DE MELÓN. POR DARME
LOS REGALOS MÁS LINDO—TU AMOR, TU GRACIA, TU PACENCIA,
Y TODO LO QUE UNA HIJA NECESITA PARA TRIUNFAR EN ESTA
VIDA. Y POR SUPUESTO, POR LAS ENSEÑANZAS DE LA COCINA.*

FOR YOU, MOTHER, MY PRECIOUS SWEETHEART.
FOR GIVING ME THE MOST PRECIOUS GIFTS: YOUR LOVE,
YOUR GRACE, YOUR PATIENCE AND EVERYTHING A DAUGHTER
NEEDS TO SUCCEED IN LIFE. AND, OF COURSE, FOR TEACHING
ME THE SOUL OF A KITCHEN.

CONTENTS

No Pressure! Desserts — 185

INTRODUCTION
Cooking Under Pressure

The cracked, eggshell-colored timer is ticking but I can't really make out the numbers, they're so faded. I've detailed the dial position, so it looks like there are seven minutes left.

"¡Mami, no le falta mucho al rabo! Qué rico huele!" ("Mami, the oxtails are almost done! Ooh, they smell so, so good!")
"No te vayas acercar más. ¡Te lo he dicho!" ("I've told you already, don't get close!")

I was seven or eight the first time I remember begging my mother to let me help her in the kitchen. She was making oxtails for dinner, a special dish reserved for special occasions. The aroma was so bold, it permeated the house, meandering its way outside. That's always been the general consensus among visiting family and friends—you knew Mami was throwing down when the smell reached our Washington, D.C. suburb, half-moon driveway. The flavored steam was coming out of a heavy stainless-steel pot whose dinged-up wooden handles were deeply scorched and cracked. I wanted to get closer to the stove as the timer approached zero, but the little dancing jiggler was making a lot of noise and I wasn't sure if it was going to pop off when the timer rang. Plus, my mother had remarkable timing. She came back into the kitchen just a few seconds before the chiming faded into the steady hissing. It was intense. She moved so swiftly from the stove to the sink, nudging me along and out of the way with her hip. She placed the cooker in the middle of the sink and gently placed a butter knife underneath the jiggler, slightly tilting it. Instantly, the hissing got louder and an aggressive flow of steam shot up toward the angled ceiling. My eyes got rounder than a tarsier's and I jerked a few steps back. I was amazed. After about a minute, she quickly tapped down the jiggler with the knife.

11

That was my first experience with the pressure cooker. It wasn't until I was twelve or so that my mother finally indulged my curiosity and invited me to watch the process from beginning to end. One of our first collaborative efforts was making *garbanzos*, her favorite dish. I didn't quite immediately grasp the concept of cooking a full dish in a tightly sealed pot, never to be opened until it was done, but I conjectured it had a special quality. She swore by that distressed pot every day. It was the one cooking gadget that mystified me and also represented our eating experience at home. It seemed as though everything she made for our family of seven came out of that single *olla*.

Her food was and still is so delicious, carrying consistent savory notes. And she seemed to cook a lot of food in a short amount of time. Dinner for an active family in one hour had me thinking Mami was Superwoman. That, or there was definitely something unique about her pressure cooker. I wanted to know what it was. Over time, I realized one of its benefits was the amount of time allocated to our daily, formal sit-down dinner. She whipped up the food so fast, our time at the table was always relaxing, inspired by animated storytelling and filled with a lot of laughter. That concentrated time she so perfectly orchestrated with her love is the foundation of our family today.

Since then, I've been enamored with this "old-school" way of cooking, learning the intricacies and mechanisms of the very thing my mother so carefully kept at bay from my hands. She eventually encouraged me to practice with her supervision.

For years, my personal goal was to master her beans. Other recipes I studied took forever. A bag of dried black beans can easily take up to three hours to cook in a traditional pot, even if you soak them overnight. In the pressure cooker, those same black beans are softened and flavored in 25 minutes if you pre-soak them. A time saving of up to 70 percent is worthy of sharing with anyone interested in cooking. I set out to do that about twelve years ago, when I finally mastered her beans.

Thanks to my mother, who still cooks that ridiculously great oxtail and those famous beans in the same pressure cooker I used to gaze at—now missing an entire handle—my experience in pressure-cooking has defined the way I function in the kitchen. It has also taught me to love and respect food in a way I can only show you by sharing a small but robust personal collection of recipes.

I carefully developed the recipes in this cookbook using modern pressure cookers—both stovetop and electric— with the purpose of reintroducing a valuable cooking method that both honors our mothers and encourages dedicated family dinnertime, an essential routine to fostering healthy relationships. And, of course, to inspire you to cook delicious dishes and meals in far less time! Cooking doesn't have to be so laborious; rather, an explorative and rewarding journey. Food is life, right?!

Each of these recipes tells a story. My philosophy is that we intimately connect with food if we understand where it comes from or what inspired it. Food is the conduit to a person's soul. It has a romantic way of connecting humans. After all, food is universal. It transcends time and culture. The recipes in this book range from delicate soups to gutsy creations like chickpea and tripe stew, one of my absolute favorite dinners while growing up! Don't let offal discourage you. You will love it. Padma Lakshmi from Top Chef does! Chapter 5, "Classic and Fusion Plates from My Cuban Kitchen," will give you a personal look at the diverse culture from which I come, sprinkled with old recipes my late grandmother in Havana passed down to my mother and that are now considered family heirlooms—recipes only my mother's hand can make blindly and still render

us submissive to her time. Those are the ones closest to my heart. I anticipated writing this book one day and decided to hold off from sharing that ridiculously perfect peppered oxtail recipe until now. I've had countless friends, colleagues and even online strangers ask for that *Rabo Encendido* recipe. It hurt me not to, but I'm so thrilled to share it now. I hope you lose your mind for a split second when you make it!

Pressure cooking has changed. Anyone can use a pressure cooker. Hissing jigglers are a true thing of the past. Exploding beans are inconceivable, thank God. Because, yes, I've seen that happen twice in my lifetime. Lord have mercy! Vigorously cleaning beans from the walls and ceiling (and cabinetry hinges) has to be the most unsatisfying time spent in the kitchen. So, I've set a new goal. I want to inspire you to cook more, to learn a new skill, to explore and to expand your repertoire by cooking delicious and new foods significantly faster. Whether the pot is vintage or new, or the cook wiser or younger, pressure cooking is a brilliant technique that will change your life. I promise.

When you taste that robust braised roast or make a decadent flan in just fifteen minutes flat, you will fall in love with pressure cooking the way I did as a child. Ultimately, I hope you are so excited to share it with your family and friends, and join me in spreading the pressure cooking gospel.

MY 5-POINT PITCH
FOR PRESSURE COOKING

TIME EFFICIENCY

Cooking with a pressure cooker can save up to 70 percent of the time spent cooking foods that would conventionally take hours.

ENERGY EFFICIENCY

Pressure cooking is a great way to reduce your carbon footprint in a growing unhealthy environment that begs conservation. The lifetime durability of a pressure cooker makes it ideal for requiring fewer utensils, not to mention significantly less use of water, gas and electricity.

BETTER-TASTING FOOD

Fresh, seasonal, nouveau and trendy food is on the up and up! Everyone wants to be a foodie, loosely defined as an "unofficial expert and food lover" in the know of what's hot and what's not, how to infuse exotic ingredients and cuisines, how to source food and even how to plate. The pressure cooker hands you a license to easily become a true expert in all of those things, even if only at home.

PERFECT FOR COLLEGE STUDENTS

Pressure cookers are incredibly practical for college students looking for easy, fast, healthy and delicious food in the comfort of their off-campus living or dorms (using an electric pressure cooker, in this case). Parents, you can save time and money if your kids have a tool that allows them to cook an endless variety of meals.

REFINING YOUR SKILLS

Pressure cooking is a science and technique. Spending time practicing and learning the few bells and whistles will inspire you to step outside of the cooking lane where you've been meandering for years. You will fall in love exploring foods you've shied away from because they took forever to cook and enjoy. Not anymore! This is modern pressure cooking.

THE PRESSURE COOKER
Then & Now

Some of my most esteemed chef friends and bona fide food experimentalists abide by the idea that all great cooking techniques, regardless of the cuisine, are based on the French model and philosophy. I didn't always agree. For me, there was little to envy from the modern Anglo-European kitchen when I considered the ancient methods discovered by the Mayans, the aboriginal peoples of Australia, neighboring Pacific nations and archaic ethnic groups in general, all of which have contributed to the love affair and respect for food modern society has. That was until I became intimately involved with the pressure cooker and explored its origins beyond my Cuban connection. It is true, indeed, that the French are responsible for dishing some of cooking's best applications. At least in the realm of speed-cooking. While indigenous methods (pit fires and slow-cooking) resolved the absence of electricity and tools, a French man discovered that food could be cooked significantly faster using steam pressure.

In 1679, physicist Denis Papin—a dedicated inventor—figured out that an airtight vessel—the Papin Steam Digester—could quickly increase water's boiling point when steam pressure was created. After a few explosions, he invented the safety valve to prevent more accidents.

The pressure cooker, initially known as the steam digester, is invented by Denis Papin.

1679

1860 Cast-iron pressure cookers are built.

Georg Gutbrod begins manufacturing pressure cookers made of tinned cast iron.

1864

1919 Jose Alix Martínez from Spain is the first person to patent the pressure cooker. He calls it la olla exprés, or the express cooker.

Germany boasts to pioneer the first mass manufacture and sale of pressure cookers.

1927

1938 Alfred Vischer Jr. designs the first personal, home-use pressure cooker. He later presents it at the 1939 New York World's Fair.

Presto Pressure Cookers produces the world's first commercial pressure cooker.

1939

1940 World War II forces a suspension in production of personal pressure cookers so manufacturing efforts and resources can focus on warfare.

America enjoys a resurgence of the pressure cooker after the ending of the war settles nerves. People are eager to live healthier lives.

1945–1950

1970 A health-conscious movement spikes sales as people are again eager to live healthier lives.

Baby boomers are revisiting their mothers' kitchen artillery and learning the benefits of pressure cooking. New models with safety valves and locks are introduced, eliminating the dancing regulator of earlier midcentury models and minimizing fear.

1991

2010–PRESENT

Stovetop cookers continue to evolve and offer more efficiency and faster cooking times, while electric cookers make waves with their "hit it and quit" one-touch technology.

BACK TO BASICS
The Essentials Before You Get Started

HOW PRESSURE COOKERS WORK

The science behind pressure cooking is quite simple. The mechanics of the lid, inclusive of a rubber gasket that fits in a groove right below the lid, creates a tight seal, allowing the water to boil at higher temperatures. Steam is compressed and trapped as it builds. The atmospheric pressure rises by 15 pounds (6.8 kg) per square inch (2.5 cm), or PSI. At the highest pressure point, water boils at 250°F (120°C), hence faster cooking times. The trapped steam also means the normal process of evaporation is diminished, maintaining higher levels of moisture in the food.

By default and generally speaking, older and newer stovetop models are preset at 15 PSI, also referred to as "high pressure." Once the cooker has reached the highest pressure point, a stem will pop up, letting you know your desired pressure has arrived. Low pressure can be considered 8–11 PSI. Some go as low as 6. It just depends on your model.

Always, *always* check your pressure cooker manual for its particular pressure settings. Not all are created equal, let me tell you. There are some stovetop models with only one setting: high. You should know that once the pressure point is reached, a safety or release valve will slightly open so that a steady flow of steam escapes while maintaining the right temperature and amount of pressure needed in the cooker. They're smart, right? This bright technology will keep you from overcooking foods (let's hope) or inviting those vintage explosions.

LET THE PRESSURE OUT!

Properly releasing pressure is a crucially important process in cooking with the pressure cooker. It's also a matter of safety when dealing with crazy hot steam pushing its way out of the cooker. Generally, most modern cookers have three ways to release pressure: natural-release, auto-release and quick-release. For purposes of addressing vintage models, cookers with a single setting (15 PSI) and a jiggler or regulator do not have an auto-release position. However, after many years of using a variety of my older models, I've safely learned how to tilt the regulator enough to place a butter knife underneath it to initiate the release, but only after I've removed the cooker from the stove. This takes serious experience, confidence and intimate knowledge of your cooker. Do not try this at home, even if you are experienced with older models. I will say it again for the sake of all our lives . . . do not ever try this at home if you have a vintage cooker.

Natural-release: Using this method allows the pressure to do its thing. Pressure will release on its own and can take anywhere between 5 and 20 minutes, depending on the quantity and density of food in the cooker. Most of the recipes in this book take no more than 10 to 12 minutes. This extra time can be useful to finish cooking such foods as beans, stocks, certain meats and large chickens. Patience is required for sure. As a rule of thumb, if pressure is still present after 10 minutes, in most cases you can turn the valve to the auto-release position, which is explained next.

Auto-release: This is a manually initiated position, which speeds up the release process. This is especially good for soups, stews, certain meats and foods requiring two rounds of cooking. Don't use this method when cooking vegetables (mostly if low quantity) as it'll actually end up cooking them even more and possibly may overcook them. Depending on your model, turn the operating valve to the auto-release position, typically depicted by a flow of steam on the dial. When releasing pressure this way, please make sure the valve is facing away from you, as the steam is coming out full throttle and really hot. I do not want you burn yourself in the process.

Quick-release: This method really underscores the benefits of pressure cooking but it mostly applies to stovetop models. It also may require a bit of practice or confidence. Quick-release almost immediately lets out all of the pressure. For stovetop models, place the cooker in the sink and run a thin stream of cold water over the closed lid. This method stops the cooking process and forces out the pressure and tempers it internally. The food is settled in one place and is no longer in an "agitated" state of dancing around. When the pressure is out, you will hear a heavy sound of decompression or a big thrusting pop, and possibly see a billowing cloud of steam, depending on your cooker. For electric pressure cookers, simply turn it off and unplug it. This method is especially necessary for more delicate foods, such as vegetables, or when there is a second round of applied pressure. But some notes on this method: If you're using a stovetop pressure cooker, don't ever run water directly over the valve or open the cooker while the water is running. Simply return the cooker back to the stove once all of the pressure is out. Also, don't submerge your cooker in water. Ever. Okay? And finally, don't ever place your electric cooker on the range.

Most modern stovetop cookers have an indicator pin that will depress or lower, letting you know all of the pressure is out. Depending on your model, slide the lock down and twist the handle to open. The beauty of modern pressure cookers is their renewed safety measure and protection. You simply can't force open a modern cooker if any pressure remains inside.

And, most electric cookers will also have the pin that depresses or lowers to indicate all of the pressure is out. If it doesn't have a pin, the safety lock will sound lightly to let you know the cooker is now ready to open.

In all cases, refer to your cooker's manual for its unique settings and pressure-release methods.

Here's a cheat-sheet graph to help you visually understand how releasing pressure works. Consider it an instaguide!

RELEASE METHOD NAME	RELEASE TYPE	TIME PRESSURE TAKES TO RELEASE		KINDS OF FOOD	RELEASE METHOD	
		Stovetop	Electric		Stovetop	Electric
Quick-Release	Immediate/ Instant	0 to 30 seconds	N/A	Small amounts of tender foods; vegetables; dishes requiring a second round of pressure	Transfer closed pressure cooker to the sink and run a thin stream of cold water over the cooker, but away from the valve.	N/A
Auto-Release	Really Fast	1 to 2 minutes	3 to 4 minutes	Beans needing a second round of pressure; certain meats or dense foods	Turn or open the knob or valve to the left or right, all the way to the release position depicted by a flow of steam.	
Slow Auto-Release	Fast	4 to 5 minutes	5 to 6 minutes	Pasta; certain rice; certain meats; oats	Turn to slightly open the valve with a controlled pulsing every 10 to 15 seconds.	
Natural-Release	Slow	5 to 15 minutes	10 to 30 minutes	Certain desserts; soups; meats; poultry after second round of cooking	Do nothing. Let the pressure out on its own; a pin will depress to alert that pressure is out.	Cancel the cooking setting. Do nothing else.

ALTITUDE COOKING

Something else to consider when using a pressure cooker is altitude. At sea level, water boils at 212°F (100°C), the standard used to calculate cooking times. For every 500-foot (152-m) increase in altitude, the boiling point decreases by 1°F (0.6°C). The atmosphere is lighter because it has less oxygen and pressure, causing moisture to quickly evaporate. Therefore, the higher you are, the longer it will take your food to cook since the water boils at much lower temperatures. Naturally, this affects cooking times and sometimes even the entire recipe. Without a pressure cooker, water cannot exceed its boiling point, so cooking over higher temperatures will not cook your food faster.

Another general rule for you: If you are cooking in high altitudes, your food will take longer to cook. Even at high pressure (15 PSI), allow your food anywhere from 5 to 15 additional minutes, as the water is still taking a bit longer to boil than if you were at sea level. Increase your time by 5 to 6 percent for every 1,000 feet (305 m) above sea level. Refer to your cooker's manual for recommended altitudes. All in all, pressure cooking is super ideal for high-altitude home cooks.

U.S. VS. INTERNATIONAL USE

Pressure cooking's popularity in the early nineteenth century settled around the world pretty firmly. In India, much as in Latin America, pressure cookers were identified as the most indispensable cooking tool, as electricity, fuel and energy were limited and rationed. Pressure cooking offered efficient cooking times, reducing the stress of not knowing when stable energy would be available for more conventional cooking.

In Cuba, specifically, the pressure cooker was simply a necessary extension of its sociopolitical nature. Dried beans, rice and certain root tubers, such as yuca, all of which were rationed and distributed by the government, were/are almost impossible to cook without the cooker. Those foods became the staple. Naturally, dried beans are cheap and yield enough to feed a family of four. The scarcity and unpredictable availability of continuous electricity made it necessary to use an appliance that cooked food much faster. The pressure cooker in Cuba also represents a political tango. In 2005, former president Fidel Castro promised to distribute 100,000 (Cuba is an island of 11 million people) government-commissioned cookers at a fraction of the cost of privately manufactured cookers, known to be made of cheap aluminum. Not only were the government-issued ones more affordable, claims of superior energy efficiency established a dependency on government assistance. Today, still, using pressure cookers in Cuba is akin to using gas on a stove.

The United States, however, has had a more fickle relationship with the pressure cooker. The impact and relevance in the United States historically has been inspired by trend rather than practicality. Cookers' introduction to the American home in the 1930s helped soften the pressures and financial implications of the war. Fuel and food cost concerns were globally aligned, but in the United States, the need eventually transitioned to limited interest. A more striking disparity in America's use was the lack of concentrated efforts for energy and water conservation. Other countries fought to reconcile palpable conditions, while Americans were on a mission to make life a one-button action. Enter the microwave.

It wasn't until the 1970s that the pressure cooker started to make a comeback, with the energy crisis at the beginning of the decade inciting a scare. By 1975, conservation policies and efforts inspired consciousness in personal consumption. The cooker perfectly underscored that goal. Even though it had staying power in American kitchens for years to come, most modern associations relegate it to grandmothers and the hype of cooking favorite meals in less than an hour.

And finally, recent resurgences are credited to haughty culinary trends identified by a select few authorities, the domination of high energy, competitive cooking shows casting chefs and cooks desperately pressed for time, and food purists interested in preserving family traditions. Ultimately, America's aha! moment has been revered and cemented in the cultural fabric of far less developed countries.

VINTAGE VS. MODERN

Earlier I illustrated the original designs of the cooker, which seem like a caveman's winter furnace. The science was successfully tested and enjoyed. Eventually, those impractical structures evolved in design, resulting in a more manageable stovetop cooker, easily used on electric or gas ranges.

My lobby to dispel the negative perception of the cooker, while professing my obsession with them over the last decade, has invited both favorable and questionable reactions, almost always with a reference to a mother or doting grandmother's intimate familiarity with them. Most notably, it was common practice to preserve foods by using the pressure cooker. Tomatoes, jellies and jams, and a variety of other seasonal foods were typically cooked or "canned" in jars and stored for later use. In the 1940s and '50s, the pressure cooker allowed housewives to maximize their time as they were busy maintaining the household with daily responsibilities, such as cleaning, ironing and grocery shopping. I actually read that in a manual from one of my oldest models, a 4-quart (3.8-L) Presto from 1948, which I still use. That little gem of a read depicted a stereotypical wife, eager to feed her family wonderful meals. The time-efficient method was the way of the times. However, its glory seemed to evaporate over the years.

As the pressure cooker became trendier, so did the rise of personal injury cases. Earlier models, pre-1990, did not come equipped with safety valves. Your only firewall was your knowledge of the cooker and a basic understanding of how pressure works. The jiggler, or regulator, lends an audible notification when pressure has reached its highest set point, a key element of tracking the cooking time. However, the jiggler had been a potential risk when users attempted to open the cooker with pressure still built up. Imagine the force thrusted having 15 PSI at 300°F (150°C) trapped inside a pot. Physics has told real stories of splattered beans rendering the ceiling a slat of filmy starch, linear steam burns on the forearm and even more devastating results. Ubiquitous praise eventually transitioned to condemning fear and a decline in personal home use.

While the science of pressure-cooking stands the test of time, advancements in technology have produced accident-proof cookers that any level of cook can use and enjoy. The modern pressure cooker is engineered to protect you and your family, while producing amazing food. Modern stovetop cookers have safety locks, which prohibit opening them until 100 percent of the pressure is released. Most models also have stems that pop up and depress, letting you know pressure is reached or fully out, respectively. Depending on your model, a lot of these wonderful modern ones have two settings—low and high, or 1 (low) and 2 (high)—allowing you to determine your pressure level, giving you tremendous control. This is especially helpful when first learning to work with pressure cookers and when cooking more sensitive foods, such as oats, rice and certain desserts. I address and share some helpful techniques for you to keep in mind throughout the book. Additionally, newer models are far more efficient than our mothers' collection as they require less water and perform much faster. The results are impeccable and truly delicious.

If I have to be honest, my personal preference for casual cooking at home is my 1950s stainless-steel, one-setting cooker. I love that thing. Check it out on page 17. My mother found it for $2 (yes, two dollars!) at an estate sale. It was brand-new, so I had the pleasure of breaking it in. I swear by that beauty. Perhaps instilled by my mother's insistence on their modesty, my vintage stovetop cookers are my kitchen gems. They're not a practical preference, truly. For more intense cooking and for my professional work, I definitely use one of my modern ones. They simply do the job so much better. They eliminate a huge amount of user error, reinforcing confidence in a generation far removed from the original technique.

Lastly, the advent of instant gratification and smart living paved a natural path for the growing ubiquity of the electric cooker. This relatively new approach to pressure-cooking takes fast cooking to new heights. Preset buttons for major food groups and automatic timers and even ultraluxe models, doubling as slow cookers, help the most novice cook maximize time while conserving energy and leaving the stovetop range free and available for other tasks. I've enjoyed working with the electric ones for their "I'll do it for you" technology. Any doubts are quickly answered in the cooker's manual. Keep it by your side. Although the ability to manipulate a stovetop model is convenient and superior to that of the electric model, especially for more skilled cooks, the benefits of the electric model are worth your study. It is a fantastic cooker for superbusy cooks not really interested in getting to know the intricacies of stovetop models.

IT'S ELECTRIC!

These savvy machines are the new IT in trendy cooking! Anyone can pressure-cook with these "hit it and quit it"–style cookers. Old, young, novice and experienced cooks all rave about the "plug it, set and go!" ease they offer. There are some nuances I want you to take note of when working with an electric cooker. Every brand and model works differently and may have varying settings, including different PSI levels. Here's my favorite general rule again: Always refer to your pressure cooker's manual for instructions on how to get started or for specific questions not addressed in this book.

From my exhaustive personal use and testing, electric cookers are very, very efficient. They almost literally do it all for you. Some of them allow you to set a timer to start cooking at a specific time. However, in all their goodness, they can take up to 30 percent more time than a stovetop cooker to reach the highest pressure point. As I noted earlier, most stovetop models are set to 15 PSI for high. Electric cookers can be set as low as 1.5 PSI and usually cap off at 11, maybe even 13. These lower pressure points will impact your cooking time if you are working with a recipe written for stovetop models. It's always a good idea to familiarize yourself with your model's manual for cooking times and conversions for various foods.

Here's a quick example: If a stovetop recipe reads to cook on high pressure and for 30 minutes over high heat, the total cook time will be 30 minutes, including the time it took to build pressure but not including the steam-release time. Keep this in mind. It works. In the electric cooker, the translation is to use the manual button to set to high pressure and to manually adjust to 30 minutes or more, depending on the food. The cook time in electric cookers is considered to begin at the time the set pressure is reached. Most cookers will have a digital timer where you can see the preheating time, followed by the countdown (the beginning of the cook time). Depending on the amount of food and density in the electric cooker, the same 30-minute stovetop cooker total time can be up to 50 minutes in an electric cooker, not including the steam-release time.

Unless otherwise noted, all sautéing for the recipes in this book is done in the cooker. If your electric pressure cooker does not have a sauté function, you can use the meat or browning setting and reduce the time by about 1 minute, as these settings are generally preset about 70–75°F (21–24°C) hotter.

MY TESTING APPROACH AND COOKING TIMES

For the recipes in this cookbook, I used 6-quart (5.7-L) and 10-quart (9.7-L) stovetop pressure cookers, one with a low (8 PSI) and a high (15 PSI) setting and the other with only a high (15 PSI) setting. General electric cooker directions are also offered for each recipe based on a multicooker with low (5–8 PSI) and high pressure (10–12 PSI) options. While times are approximate for both stovetop and electric, always consider your range as electric and gas invariably conduct differently in addition to your cooker's own settings. Recipes with potentially extra cooking times are marked within the instructions or have notes. Pay attention to those. Again, I encourage you throughout this book to always refer to your own cooker's manual for operational or technical questions. I'm not overboard with it, but I really can't emphasize it enough.

Here's another instaguide for quick reference. This graph lists pressure levels and cook times for some of the major food groups and some dishes within those groups. This will help as you grow in your pressure cooking journey. But you know what I'm going to suggest again: Check your pressure cooker's manual for its suggested cook times for certain foods if you're looking for something specific.

QUICK GUIDE TO COOK TIMES FOR COMMON FOODS			
VEGETABLES	STOVETOP (IN MINUTES)	ELECTRIC (IN MINUTES)	PRESSURE LEVEL
Artichoke	9–13	11–15	High
Broccoli	2–3	3–4	High
Brussels sprouts	5–8	6–9	High
Carrots, 1 inch (2.5 cm)	4–5	5–6	High
Cauliflower	2–4	3–5	High
Corn on the cob	3–4	4–5	High
Green beans, whole	3–4	4–5	High
Okra	3–4	4–5	High
Potatoes	5–7	7–9	High
Pumpkin	3–5	4–6	High
Spinach	2	2	High
Swiss chard	2–3	2–3	High

QUICK GUIDE TO COOK TIMES FOR COMMON FOODS (CONTINUED)			
BEANS (BASED ON ONE DRY CUP)	STOVETOP (IN MINUTES)	ELECTRIC (IN MINUTES)	PRESSURE LEVEL
White	5–8	8–11	High
Black	8–12	12–16	High
Chickpeas	12–14	16–18	High
Lentils	7–10	9–12	High
Green split peas	9–12	10–13	High
Red beans	20–25	25–35	High
GRAINS	STOVETOP (IN MINUTES)	ELECTRIC (IN MINUTES)	PRESSURE LEVEL
White rice (2 cups [421 g])	8–11	11–14	Low
Brown rice (2 cups [370 g])	15–20	20–25	High
Risotto (2 cups [422 g])	10–13	14–17	High
MEAT & POULTRY	STOVETOP (IN MINUTES)	ELECTRIC (IN MINUTES)	PRESSURE LEVEL
Beef brisket/roast (1½ lbs [680 g])	30–45	35–50	High
Flank steak (1½ lbs [680 g])	30	35	High
Beef tongue (2 lbs [907 g])	60	70	High
Meatballs (1 lb [453 g])	5–8	9–12	High
Pork roast (1½ lbs [680 g])	25	30	High
Pork shoulder (1½ lbs [680 g])	30–35	35–45	High
Lamb leg (2 lbs [907 g])	35–40	40–45	High

(continued)

QUICK GUIDE TO COOK TIMES FOR COMMON FOODS (CONTINUED)			
MEAT & POULTRY (CONTINUED)	STOVETOP (IN MINUTES)	ELECTRIC (IN MINUTES)	PRESSURE LEVEL
Oxtails (2 lbs [907 g])	30–40	35–45	High
Lamb shank (2½ lbs [1.13 kg])	30–35	35–40	High
Chicken, whole (2 lbs [907 g])	12–15	15–20	High
Chicken, pieces (2 lbs [907 g])	8–12	12–16	High
Chicken stock (2 qts [1.9 L])	45–50	50–60	High
Beef stock (2 qts [1.9 L])	60	60–70	High
CUSTARDS/ FRUIT DESSERTS	STOVETOP (IN MINUTES)	ELECTRIC (IN MINUTES)	PRESSURE LEVEL
Flan (1 qt [946 ml])	10–15	15–18	High
Bread pudding (1 qt [946 ml])	12	15–18	High
Cheesecake (7-inch [17-cm])	17	20–23	High
Pears, halved (5 lbs [2.3 kg])	8–10	8–10	High
Apples, halved (5 lbs [2.3 kg])	6–8	6–8	High
Papaya (1 large)	10	10	High

CHECKING FOR DONENESS

In some cases, cooking an extra 2 to 5 minutes is necessary to achieve proper or desired doneness. To check for doneness, turn off your cooker (most electric models have a "cancel" button) and apply auto-release to let the pressure out. If your food needs to be cooked a little longer, close the lid and reset the cooker and set to 4 to 5 minutes total on high pressure. The cooker will already be hot, and therefore will reach pressure very fast. Alternatively, and depending on what you're cooking, you can simply transfer your food to a conventional pot and finish cooking on the range.

KEY GADGETRY

The beauty of using a pressure cooker as a main cooking vessel is the minimalistic inventory you need. The pressure cooker, on a basic level, serves as a regular pot. In it, you can sear, sauté, brown, boil and simmer solids and liquids you will need for any pressure-cooked recipes. I'm not suggesting you don't need other skillets, pots and pans—those are necessary. However, the diversity of the cooker allows you to streamline your needs. Also, starting an entire recipe in the cooker, when permissible, ensures an added layer of flavor not so immediately accomplished otherwise. That said, here are some cooking essentials I find extremely useful when cooking and developing your skills. These specifically will accompany your pressure cooker as you cook through this book.

Cake mold (7-inch [18-cm] diameter): *Use this for making cakes that will serve four to six. A 6- to 8-inch (15- to 20.5-cm) diameter mold will fit into a 6- to 10-quart (5.7- to 9.5-L) stovetop and electric pressure cooker.*

Cheese grater: *Use this to shred cheese to different sizes. A top-handle grater is great for shredding big blocks of cheese.*

Cheesecloth: *Ideal for straining, cleaning, covering, steaming and basting food. Use to keep seeds out when squeezing fresh citrus juice into food. Cheesecloth is also wonderful for wrapping poached foods and herbal packs.*

Flan mold (1 quart [946 ml]), or similar mold: *This stainless-steel mold is ideal for making a flan recipe from beginning to end as you can make the caramel inside the mold and then add the custard mixture. Three latches secure your custard inside while cooking in the pressure cooker. You can find 1½-quart (1.4-L) molds for a bigger flan. Your best bet is to search online.*

Food processor: *These crafty tools are a must for breaking down hard foods, perfectly combining mixes and blending or puréeing sauces and soups. A handful of recipes in this book require processing. You can also use a high-powered blender if you don't have a processor.*

Immersion blender: *This is probably one of my favorite countertop appliances. This is what you want to use to easily purée soups, pulverize fruits and chop large quantities of hard foods, such as ice and nuts. Immerse it in your pressure cooker to purée some of the featured soup recipes in this book.*

Inexpensive kitchen towels: *If you cook regularly, kitchen towels are indispensable. Ikea has really basic ones for 78 cents. I use them for everything, from cleaning and wiping to wrapping certain foods cooked in the pressure cooker, specifically the Old-School, New-School Poached Cuban-Style Meat Loaf (page 67). Stock up on these.*

Kitchen timer: *If you work with a stovetop pressure cooker, you will need one of these to set cooking times. Alternatively, a smartphone's speech-to-text works brilliantly.*

Ladle: *Small and large ladles are common in commercial kitchens to pour liquids into a cooking vessel as much as over the top of a finished dish. A ladle offers quantity and quality (presentation) control in sauced foods.*

Long fork: *A long fork is great for placing and removing large pieces of protein in and out of pressure cookers. It's also great for piercing certain meats during the seasoning process.*

Metal whisk: *Use whisks instead of a fork to whisk or whip food. Its shape, whether balloon, flat or other, will create air and add fluffiness to your food.*

Microplane, zester: *Zest from citrus fruits adds an incredible amount of flavor to food, especially pastries and desserts. These simple hand tools will scrape the zest of lemons, limes, oranges, grapefruit and anything having* flavedo *(white flesh).*

Mini hand strainer or sieve: *A smaller wire or plastic strainer will easily and comfortably separate smaller particles and quantity foods, such as egg whites in custard, spice seeds and sparse broths/stocks.*

Mortar and pestle: *Use this combination to break down smaller ingredients, such as garlic, and pulverize such spices as cloves, cumin and coriander. Rock or marble mortar and pestles are most common. Wooden ones are great for maintaining the integrity of flavor. All are great for making spice blends. I recommend a wooden one if a recipe calls for adding oil.*

Pressure cooker tray: *Every pressure cooker should come with a tray for placing smaller vessels inside. A tray is required for steaming inside the cooker.*

Ramekins: *Use ceramic or glass ramekins to make individual dishes and desserts in the pressure cooker. It is safe to cover ramekins with a single layer of aluminum foil while cooking.*

Silicone gloves: *Most silicone products have a heat resistance of 500°F (250°C), making them safe to use when handling extremely hot foods. Use them for removing molds from your cooker and handling cast-iron skillets.*

Slotted spoons: *These are a must for straining unwanted liquids in beans, rice, grains and similar dishes.*

Tongs: *Tongs are your extended hands when handling and transferring raw meat. They are also very handy for turning foods while cooking.*

Twine: *Cotton kitchen string is used to tie together and hold in place large foods, such as the legs on a whole chicken. It is also used for tying smaller foods, such as tamales and herbs.*

Wooden spoons, large and small: *I'm a fan of wooden spoons and their natural composition, which lends to enjoying the full integrity of food. Steel and other metal ware can transfer particles and potentially alter taste. Maintain them with olive oil or other wood oils.*

B IN THE KNOW!

— A FEW TIPS TO KEEP IN MIND WHILE YOU COOK ALONG —

Making Sofrito

This is the glorious flavor base in Latin cooking. In Cuban cuisine, we call it the "Holy Trinity," usually a mix of onions, garlic and bell pepper. There are many variations, but making a *sofrito* generally consists of sautéing vegetables in hot oil and seasoning with dried spices and herbs, which produces a very fragrant sauce. The French call it a *mire poix*, with carrots and celery. I use a *sofrito* in almost all of my meat and bean recipes and some others throughout. Where some would just add all of the ingredients in the cooker at once, starting with a *sofrito* guarantees a solid base layer of flavor to build on. For purposes of this book, if a recipe says, "make the *sofrito*," it refers to sautéing the vegetables with seasonings (if noted) before the next step.

Serving Amounts

Most of the recipes are made with four to six servings in mind. However, some of them yield enough for six to eight and in fewer cases eight to ten. Those larger-quantity ones are especially useful for foods that would take significantly longer if cooked conventionally, namely beans and collard greens. A larger amount for those foods is more efficient and convenient in that most can be frozen for a long time, generally speaking.

The Use of That Little Sazón Seasoning Packet

It is very true that those little packets of seasoning are ubiquitous and a basic ingredient in Latin cooking. Over time, it has become popular with home cooks looking to add extra flavor to savory food, regardless of cooking style or cuisine. It's also true that it has a bit of MSG, leading some to make their own blend. For the sake of debate, which I've been subjected to, I left Sazón out of all the recipes I'd normally use it in when cooking at home. That said, I encourage you to try it! There is a wide range of Sazón blends. The ones with achiote are used to give foods an orange or yellow hue, such as the Vibrant Yellow Vegetable Rice (page 93). The ones without achiote don't have the coloring in them and thus can be used in everything else. If you choose to add a packet to a recipe, lessen the salt in the recipe by one-quarter, depending on your palate.

The Skinny on Sauces

Not all braising and pot sauces are created equal; there are times when a thicker sauce is absolutely necessary for the dish to really sing. Reducing sauces concentrates their flavor profile and empowers the dish, whether it's for beef, poultry or even syrups for desserts. Ideally, a well-rounded sauce will have the consistency of a velvety layer that covers the back of a spoon without too much dripping. A perfectly reduced sauce will require simmering and not really reaching a boil. For the purposes of this book and the speedy recipes, most reductions are done over medium to high heat for 10 minutes or so, depending on the sauce and the amount in the cooker. If you are using an electric pressure cooker, you can reduce the sauce using the simmer function (200°F [93°C]) for a longer time, or bring to a boil using the steam function (212°F [100°C]). In any case, whether noted or not, feel free to reduce to your liking.

Coloring with a Vibrant Flower Oil

Saffron is beautiful, but it's very expensive and potentially an acquired taste. I love it and use it here and there in some of the recipes in this book. However, if you're not feeling it but still want or need to achieve a beautiful red, burnt orange color, make your own coloring agent with achiote (definition on page 212). Warm ⅓ cup (80 ml) of good olive oil and add 1 tablespoon (6 g) of achiote seeds. Allow to infuse until the color is deep and rich, about 30 to 45 seconds, and then strain. Use this in lieu of saffron or to color risotto, rice and certain meats. Just make sure to add additional seasoning to make up for the omitted saffron. Or, simply use to add color.

GET STARTED WITH THESE STARTERS, APPS AND SIDES

Appetizers are underrated. We go out to eat and order them because we're hungry or need to fill the time spent catching up with our family and friends. I've not done any empirical research but I wonder if there's any correlation between the appetizers we order and the ensuing enjoyment of the rest of the courses. I want to argue appetizers can make or break our palate, ultimately defining our dining experience. After all, typically, they are the first thing we bite into. I love appetizers so much I have to be careful in measuring myself. I want them to be really good, but not so filling I won't eat a main course. That brings me to the appetizers in this book. My goal is twofold: to ease you into pressure cooking with easy dishes that'll intrigue you to meander through the process; and to offer you really good starters versatile enough to enjoy any time of day. These dishes are quite simple and illustrate how fast you can cook delicious food. I can eat any of these on their own or paired with something more elaborate. The plantain mash is an upgraded version of a simple Cuban dish that doubles as a starchy side or filling accompaniment to a nice cut of meat. Fall scents of cinnamon, nutmeg and cloves in that sweet dish will turn it into a regular option for you and your family. My absolute favorite, however, is the first recipe, the Sweet English Pea and Mint Soup (page 32). Once you make and try it in fifteen minutes, you'll agree on its lead placement!

SWEET ENGLISH PEA AND MINT SOUP

I loathed peas while growing up, even though they were incorporated in a lot of our rice dishes. We call them *petits pois*, or little peas. I used to pick them out of everything they landed on. During a trip to Prague in the spring, I had the most remarkable chilled pea soup for breakfast at a coffee bar. It was bright and light in consistency and paired well with my coffee, oddly enough. A crazy combination, I know, but it's lingered in my heart since then and converted me into a pea fan. But only in the soup form. This vibrant soup was inspired by that visit, with a touch of added creaminess and herbal elegance. Enjoy it cold or warm. I love it warm with crusty bread. No coffee, please.

SERVES 4 TO 6

1 tbsp (14 g) unsalted butter

1 cup (60 g) chopped spring onions

2 cloves garlic, minced

3 fresh sage leaves, minced,
or 2 tsp (1.5 g) dried

½ cup (60 g) all-purpose flour

2 cups (475 ml) Herbed Chicken Stock
(page 166), or store-bought

3 cups (450 g) English peas, preferably fresh

7–8 fresh mint leaves, rubbed and chopped

1 tsp (6 g) kosher salt

⅛ tsp freshly ground white pepper

1 tsp (5 ml) vegetable oil

½ cup (70 g) unsalted pumpkin seeds,
plus more for garnish

Sea salt

1¼ cups (285 ml) light whipping cream

3 tbsp (9 g) thinly sliced fresh chives,
for garnish

Melt the butter in the pressure cooker over medium heat for the stovetop pressure cooker or use the sauté setting for the electric pressure cooker. Add the spring onions, garlic, sage and flour, in that order. Whisk constantly, making sure the flour doesn't clump, about 3 minutes. Stir in the chicken stock. Cook for an additional 3 minutes. Add the peas and mint. Season with the kosher salt and the pepper. Cancel cooking for the electric cooker, and close the lid.

Stovetop: Set to high pressure (15 PSI) and cook over medium heat for 6 minutes total.

Electric: Use the soup setting, or set to high pressure (10–12 PSI) and 8 minutes.

When done, remove from the heat or turn off the cooker and release the pressure, using auto-release.

While the peas are cooking, toast the pumpkin seeds: Heat the oil over medium in a small skillet. Add the pumpkin seeds and season with sea salt to taste. Toast the seeds, turning on each side until they are browned but not burned, about 3 minutes. Remove from the heat and set aside.

When all of the pressure is out, stir in the whipping cream. Purée using an immersion blender or transfer the soup to a large food processor or suitable blender and purée the peas until they're smooth and velvety. If you have to, do it in two batches. Stir well and let simmer for 5 minutes. If you did this in a processor or blender, transfer the soup back to the pressure cooker, scraping it with a rubber spatula.

Serve immediately in individual bowls, or allow the soup to cool and then transfer to the refrigerator to chill. Garnish each serving with 1 tablespoon (9 g) of pumpkin seeds and chives.

Sweet Plantain Mash

Plantains, ripe or green, are one of Latin cuisine's biggest stars. Sweet fried plantains, or *platanitos fritos*, were the very first thing I learned how to fry, when I was seven. This *fufú*, a traditional mash with origins in West Africa, is typically enjoyed as a savory option for breakfast. Customarily, it is flavored with bacon and onions. My *fufú* is a result of expanding the versatility of sweet plantains. Infused with aromatic spices, this creamy mash is filling on its own.

Serves 4 to 6

4 medium-ripe plantains, peeled, cut into 2" (5-cm) pieces

3 cups (710 ml) Herbed Chicken Stock (page 166) or Simple Vegetable Broth (page 157), or store-bought

5 garlic cloves, 3 sliced and 2 minced, divided

2 tbsp (28 ml) extra-virgin olive oil, plus more for drizzling

¼ cup (55 g) butter

1 cup (235 ml) freshly squeezed orange juice

¼ tsp ground allspice

¼ tsp ground cinnamon

¼ tsp freshly grated nutmeg

1 tbsp (15 ml) honey

Salt

1 tbsp (2.5 g) minced fresh basil, for garnish

B'S COOKING TIP: Depending on the ripeness of your plantains, the mash could be a bit too dry for your taste. If it is add about ¼ cup (60 ml) of the pot broth or 1–2 teaspoons (5–10 g) of butter.

Add the plantains, broth and the 2 minced garlic cloves to the pressure cooker.

Stovetop: Set to high pressure (15 PSI) and cook over high heat for 7 minutes total.

Electric: Set to high pressure (10–12 PSI) and 10 minutes.

When done, remove from the heat or turn off the cooker and allow the pressure to release on its own (natural-release). While the plantains are cooking, prepare the garlic: In a small skillet, heat the olive oil and brown the remaining sliced garlic, about 30 seconds. Immediately remove from the heat and set aside.

When all of the pressure is out, open the cooker and strain the liquid. Allow the plantains to cool for a few minutes. Using tongs, remove the plantains and transfer to a medium mixing bowl. Mash the plantains, using a potato masher, until smooth and creamy. It's okay if you see little black seeds. Fold in the butter, orange juice, dried spices and honey. Season with salt to taste. Top with the sautéed garlic and drizzle the olive oil all over the top. You can stir well to incorporate, if you want. Garnish with the basil. Serve immediately.

*See photo on page 30.

HOW TO CHOOSE PLANTAINS!		
RIPENESS	WHAT TO LOOK FOR	COMMON USE
Green	Extra firm, solid green skin	Savory mashes, chips
Medium	Firm, light blemishing, mostly yellow with some incoming large dark brown or black spots/patches	*Tostones* (twice-fried patties), soups and stews, paper-thin slices, poached
Medium to Ripe	Soft to firm, dark yellow with dark brown or black spots or speckles	*Maduros* or fried, sweet/savory stuffed balls
Overripe	Mushy, shriveled and mostly black	Shakes. That's about it!

READY-MADE ARTICHOKES

A growing favorite appetizer or snack, the leaves of an artichoke serve as a delicate but interesting treat. We're seeing them at cocktail parties, Sunday brunches and more formal settings, for their unexpected accessibility yet intriguing eating style. Sucking and pulling on leafy grains is trendy. Imagine that. But they need some flavor assistance. I love a simple garlic "bath" that adds some sweet pungency. Cooking a few medium artichokes in fifteen minutes makes them really attractive for your next dinner party.

SERVES 4 TO 6

2 medium artichokes
1 tbsp (15 ml) lemon juice
3 cloves garlic, skin on, mashed
Leaves from 4 sprigs fennel
1 tsp (6 g) kosher salt

Cut off and discard the stem and the hard tips of the artichokes. Add the lemon juice, garlic, fennel leaves and salt to the pressure cooker and stir. Place the artichokes, facing up, in the pressure cooker and add enough water to cover them halfway. Close the lid.

Stovetop: Set to high pressure (15 PSI) and cook over high heat for 12 minutes. When the pressure is reached, lower the heat enough to maintain the pressure level and continue to cook.

Electric: Set to high pressure (10–12 PSI) and 15 minutes.

When done, remove from the heat or turn off the cooker and release the pressure, using auto-release. When all of the pressure is out, open the lid and remove the artichokes from the cooker, using tongs. Peel back the leaves to enjoy.

Serve with your favorite dip. A simple mix of olive oil or melted butter and salt is a good way to become acquainted with the purplish thistle flower.

 B IN THE KNOW! Buy fresh artichokes in season and from farmers' markets when you can. They are less expensive then and taste better, naturally.

CREAMY SPINACH ARTICHOKE DIP

Artichoke dip is that warm appetizer you can't get enough of, no matter the season. It's easily one of America's best go-to dips when entertaining at home, because of its wide appeal. It's also a suitable spread. Plus, you can really personalize this without much effort. A pinch of smoked paprika will give it an added punch. The garlic in this recipe is the star but the spice also makes it special.

SERVES 4 TO 6

5 (6-oz [170-g]) bags fresh baby spinach, or 1 (6-oz [170-g]) bag frozen, cleaned, finely chopped and patted dry

1 (8-oz [225-g]) bar cream cheese, softened

2 to 3 fresh artichoke hearts, choked and roughly chopped, or 1 (16-oz [455-g]) jar marinated hearts, drained

4 cloves garlic, crushed

2 tbsp (28 ml) hot sauce

⅓ cup (80 ml) water

1½ tsp (9 g) salt for fresh artichokes, or 1 tsp (6 g) for jarred

3 tbsp (45 ml) Italian dressing, if using fresh artichokes (optional; see notes)

Add all of the ingredients to the pressure cooker, in the order listed. Using a wooden spoon, fold the ingredients and combine well and close the lid.

Stovetop: Set to high pressure (15 PSI) and cook over high heat for 12 minutes total if using fresh artichoke hearts and 8 minutes total if using jarred.

Electric: Set to high pressure (10–12 PSI) and 10 minutes for fresh artichokes, or low pressure (5–8 PSI) and 7 minutes for jarred.

When done, remove from the heat or turn off the cooker and release the pressure, using auto-release. When all of the pressure is out, open the lid. Stir well and adjust for salt if necessary.

Serve warm. Goes well with fresh pita, toasted pita chips or toasted artisan bread you already have. Also makes for a great spread for turkey or portobello sandwiches.

 B CREATIVE! As a delicious variation, try topping the dip with shredded Parmesan cheese and bake in a preheated 375°F (190°C) oven for 10 minutes, or until the cheese is lightly browned.

 B'S COOKING TIP: Adding 3 tablespoons (45 ml) of Italian dressing provides great flavor if you are using fresh artichoke hearts. If you do, reduce the salt amount by half.

CREAMY CORN POLENTA

There are a few foods I stay away from even though I love them deeply. Polenta is one of them. This creamy cornmeal "bowl," rooted in Italian peasantry, humbly livens the adage "Less is more." It's hearty and substantially filling, making it an ideal side dish, a base for a savory stew or a mélange such as the Soulful Beef, Okra and Plantain Mélange on page 145. That's a divine combination I know you'll love. I've tweaked this version to be a wonderful and airy starter to your more complex dishes.

SERVES 4 TO 6

2½ cups (590 ml) water

1 cup (235 ml) milk, plus ½ cup (120 ml)

1 cup (235 ml) Herbed Chicken Stock (page 166), or store-bought

1 cup (140 g) stone-ground yellow cornmeal (noninstant)

2 tsp (9 g) sugar

1½ tsp (2 g) dried thyme, or 1 tsp (1 g) fresh

½ tsp achiote oil (optional)

1 cup (225 g) corn, canned (drained) or fresh

2 tbsp (28 g) salted cultured butter

1 tsp (6 g) kosher salt, or to taste

Add all of the liquid, except the ½ cup (120 ml) of milk, to the pressure cooker and stir. Bring to a very light boil over medium heat for the stovetop pressure cooker or use the sauté setting for the electric pressure cooker, about 3 minutes.

Gently whisk in the cornmeal, maintaining the low heat. Constantly stir the mixture, using a metal whisk, as it thickens and turns into polenta, about 2 minutes. Stir in the sugar and thyme, and the achiote oil if desired. Cancel cooking for the electric cooker, and close the lid.

Stovetop: Set to high pressure (15 PSI) and cook over high heat for 6 minutes total. When the pressure point has been reached, lower the heat to medium to finish cooking.

Electric: Set to high pressure (10–12 PSI) and 8 minutes total.

When done, remove from the heat or turn off the cooker and allow the pressure to release on its own (natural-release). When all of the pressure is out, open the cooker. Gently stir in the corn, remaining ½ cup (120 ml) of milk and butter. Season with salt.

Serve immediately.

B CREATIVE! For a savory polenta "cake," pour the polenta into small ramekins while still hot. The polenta will set within 5 to 10 minutes. Bake in a preheated 350°F (180°C) oven for 15 minutes. Unmold from the ramekins and serve with your favorite savory sauce.

B'S COOKING TIP: Polenta can be eaten alone or topped with your favorite savory sauce. The Soulful Beef, Okra and Plantain Mélange (page 145) is a crazy good combination if you make plain polenta without the corn. The corn is good and will add to the experience, but I love the flavors and textures of that stew with something creamier.

Asian-Spiced Turkey Meatballs

I didn't meet my maternal grandfather until I was 20 years old, and when I did, our facial similarity left me in awe. Here was this fragile, elderly man in his early 70s, rocking back and forth in a beat-up wicker chair. He was so adorable. He was so Chinese. I'd seen pictures of him while growing up but it didn't hit me until I embraced him in person: There is a visible Asian thread on both sides of my family, which I've never really explored. And though my father has always addressed my mother as "China" (little Chinese girl), a direct implication of her father, that culture sits very dormant in my life. These spicy, sweet and savory meatballs are a small way of acknowledging my mother's very authentic characteristic (and my paternal grandmother) and hopefully the beginning of a journey of delicious findings. They make a whimsical appetizer for any casual or elaborate meal. Make them a bit bigger, double the sauce and enjoy as your main protein for dinner!

YIELDS 28 SMALL TO MEDIUM MEATBALLS

Spicy Sweet-and-Sour Sauce

¼ cup (50 g) granulated sugar

¼ cup (60 g) packed light brown sugar

2 tbsp (28 ml) ketchup

2 tbsp (28 ml) soy sauce, regular or white

6 tbsp (90 ml) rice vinegar (seasoned is okay)

1 tbsp (8 g) ginger paste

½ tsp sea salt

1 cup (235 ml) water

1 tbsp (15 ml) hot sauce

4 tsp (11 g) cornstarch, plus 4 tbsp (60 ml) warm water

Meatballs

1 lb (455 g) ground turkey

½ white onion, finely minced

½ green bell pepper, finely minced

5 cloves garlic, minced

1¼ cups (285 ml) spicy sweet-and-sour sauce (recipe precedes)

1 tbsp (15 ml) Worcestershire sauce

¼ cup (60 ml) milk

½ cup (35 g) crumbled soda crackers

1 tsp (6 g) salt

1 tbsp (15 ml) sesame oil

1 tbsp (15 ml) canola oil

1 cup (235 ml) Herbed Chicken Stock (page 166), or store-bought

1 spring onion, diagonally sliced

Prepare the sweet-and-sour sauce: Add all of the sauce ingredients to a saucepan, in the order listed, except the cornstarch and warm water. Bring to a medium boil, stirring constantly. In a small bowl, mix the cornstarch and warm water to dissolve the starch. Slowly add the starch mixture to the saucepan and bring to a boil, gently stirring constantly, until the sauce thickens, about 3 minutes. Remove from the heat and set aside to allow it to cool and form. This is going to be your seasoning base and sauce.

(continued)

ASIAN-SPICED TURKEY MEATBALLS (CONT.)

Prepare the meatballs: Place the turkey, onion, bell pepper, garlic, 1 cup (235 ml) of the sweet-and-sour sauce, the Worcestershire, milk, crumbled crackers and salt in a medium mixing bowl. Gently blend with a wooden spoon until everything is well combined. Chill for 30 minutes (optional).

Using your hands, shape the mixture into 1-inch (2.5-cm) round balls. Perfection is not necessary.

Heat the sesame and canola oils in the stovetop pressure cooker over low or use the sauté setting of the electric pressure cooker.

Gently place and arrange the meatballs in the cooker. Turn up the heat to medium for the stovetop pressure cooker or cancel cooking for the electric cooker (the residual heat will continue cooking the meatballs). Lightly brown the meatballs, about 2 minutes.

In a bowl, mix the remaining ½ cup (120 ml) of sweet-and-sour sauce and the stock to combine well. Evenly pour the sauce over the meatballs. Do not stir. Close the lid.

Stovetop: Set to high pressure (15 PSI) and set the timer for 10 minutes total. Cook over high heat until the pressure point has been reached, about 7 minutes. When the pressure is reached, lower the heat to medium and finish cooking for the remaining 3 minutes.

Electric: Set to high pressure (10–12 PSI) and 12 minutes.

When done, remove from the heat or turn off the cooker and allow the pressure to release on its own (natural-release). If any pressure remains after 8 minutes, turn the valve to the auto-release position to finish.

When all of the pressure is out, transfer the meatballs to a serving platter, using a large slotted spoon. Ladle the sauce over the meatballs. Garnish with spring onions.

 B CREATIVE! This dish is packed with intense flavor as is. However, you can also make this with ground beef and/or pork and still enjoy a great appetizer.

 B'S COOKING TIP: Do note that the sweet-and-sour sauce is very spicy. If you are of low heat tolerance, like me, tone it down by reducing the hot sauce to 2 teaspoons (10 ml) from 1 tablespoon (15 ml).

SOUTHERN-STYLE SHRIMP AND GRITS

I came to know true grits only a decade ago when I moved to Atlanta, the "dirty South"! I quickly learned it had a burgeoning food scene. It's only bigger and better now but Atlantans know southern food well. I used to order cheese grits whenever I saw it on a menu. The first order I recall was spiced with jalapeño. And then I learned of shrimp and grits, a beloved breakfast and brunch dish in the South. It's the dish to order when you want a classic comfort food. Root, a restaurant in New Orleans, makes a Creole version even sexier. My mother and I visited NOLA together for the first time while I was writing this book. I insisted she try a bowl. She'd never heard of it but was there to expand her palate. Her reaction was priceless, guaranteeing an inspired recipe for you to make. She ordered four more versions during our three-day jaunt. I developed this recipe for her, to marry the flavors she loves but also to remind her of the Creole spirit she connected with. She fully approves of this!

SERVES 4

1½ lbs (680 g) shrimp

Fish Stock

3½ cups (830 ml) water

1 bay leaf

3 cloves garlic, peeled, left whole

Grits

1 cup (140 g) white or yellow stone ground grits

¼ cup (60 ml) heavy whipping cream

1 tsp (3 g) seeded and minced jalapeño pepper

1 tsp (6 g) kosher salt

1 cup (115 g) shredded extra-sharp cheddar cheese

¼ cup (20 g) shredded Parmesan cheese

1 tbsp (14 g) butter

Shrimp Sauce

3 tbsp (42 g) unsalted butter

½ cup (80 g) diced white onion

2 cloves garlic, minced

½ cup (70 g) diced green or red bell pepper

¾ cup (53 g) stemmed and sliced white or cremini mushrooms

1 cup (180 g) canned diced tomatoes and green chiles (see notes)

¼ cup (61 g) tomato sauce

1 tbsp (15 ml) Worcestershire sauce

1 tsp (5 ml) hot sauce

Salt

Juice of 1 lemon

3 scallions, diced, for garnish

Freshly ground black pepper (optional)

(continued)

Wash and peel the shrimp. Keep the shells.

To make the fish stock, add the water, shrimp shells, bay leaf and garlic to the pressure cooker and close the lid.

Stovetop: Set to high pressure (15 PSI) and cook over high heat for 6 minutes.

Electric: Set to high pressure (10–12 PSI) and 8 minutes.

When done, remove from the heat or cancel the cooker and release the pressure, using auto-release. When all of the pressure is out, open the cooker and strain, reserving all of the stock. Discard the shells and bay leaf.

To make the grits, turn the heat to low for the stovetop pressure cooker or use the simmer function for the electric pressure cooker. Add the stock back to the cooker. Gradually add the grits, stirring constantly. Slowly stir in the cream, jalapeño and salt, about 3 minutes. Cancel the simmer function for the electric cooker, and close the lid.

Stovetop: Set to high pressure (15 PSI) and set the timer for 10 minutes. Cook over high heat until pressure is reached, then lower to medium or enough to maintain pressure and continue cooking.

Electric: Set to high pressure (10–12 PSI) and 12 minutes.

While the grits are cooking, make the shrimp sauce: Warm the butter in a cast-iron skillet or medium saucepan. Sweat the onions, about 2 minutes, then add the garlic and bell peppers. Stir in the mushrooms, tomatoes and tomato sauce and cook over low-medium heat for 2 minutes. Add the shrimp, Worcestershire and hot sauce and season with salt to taste. Stir and reduce the heat to low; cook until you have achieved a slightly thick sauce, about 7 minutes. If you want to thicken it more, stir in more butter and turn the heat to medium-high until you have the right consistency. When done, squeeze fresh lemon juice over the mixture.

Stovetop: When the grits are done, remove from the heat and release the pressure, using quick-release.

Electric: Turn off the cooker and apply a quick-release by setting to auto-release and gently pulsing the valve every 10 seconds or so, until all of the pressure is released.

When all of the pressure is out, open the cooker and immediately stir the grits, gently scraping the sides. Fold in the cheeses and stir until they're melted and well incorporated. Stir in the butter until creamy. Pour the grits into individual serving bowls. Evenly distribute the shrimp and mushroom sauce with the pan juices, among the grits. Garnish with scallions.

 B'S COOKING TIPS: One (10-ounce [280-g]) can of Rotel brand tomatoes is good for this. The canned tomatoes have some heat! For a milder sauce, replace the canned tomatoes with 1 cup (150 g) of halved cherry tomatoes. Season with a bit of salt and freshly ground black pepper. The shrimp sauce is perfectly suitable on its own or as a topping for something else. The Creamy Corn Polenta on page 38 is an amazing option.

TENDER MEATS AND JUICY CHICKEN

One of the immediate benefits of pressure cooking is the preservation of nutrients and vitamins in food. Moisture retention is significantly increased since higher temperatures result in less cooking time. When it comes to cooking meat, a common dilemma is wanting the perfect combination of tender and juicy, two contradicting characteristics requiring two different temperatures. The pressure cooker easily resolves conventional cooking temperatures and yields a supertender and juicy rib or leg of lamb, and anything in between. In as little as 35 minutes, you can enjoy more than 3 pounds (1.4 kg) of pulled pork BBQ that would typically take you hours to tenderize and maintain succulent. This is the kind of talk by which a true carnivore is spell-bound! Over the years, I've increasingly relied on my pressure cookers for my tougher cuts. You will be amazed at the results and may quickly find yourself introducing new cuts and styles of food to your dinner table.

This chapter is a guide for working with more popular meats, but also cuts I've been eating my entire life, such as Your New Favorite Beef Tongue Dish on page 51. Corned beef in 50 minutes, beef tongue in 35 minutes and braised short ribs in 25 minutes are the just the beginning of what you'll master. Get busy and fret not a fatty tail.

BRAISED PULLED PORK BBQ

This supersimple, Latin-inspired pork BBQ is a one-step pot of juicy goodness. The rounded flavor profile is robust with some heat, some texture and a beautiful color. It's delicious with fluffy white rice or as a sandwich (add pickles and sliced red onions!). The one-pot, one-stir approach will keep it in constant rotation. Pat yourself on the back when you're shredding that pork in as little as 35 minutes.

SERVES 6

1½ cups (240 g) diced Spanish onion (large dice)

1 cup (150 g) diced green bell pepper (large dice)

2 Roma tomatoes, cut into large dice

4 cloves garlic, thinly sliced

¾ cup (175 ml) cider vinegar

3 tbsp (45 ml) Worcestershire sauce

1 tbsp (16 g) tomato paste

¾ cup (170 g) light or dark brown sugar

1 cup (240 g) ketchup

1½ tbsp (27 g) kosher salt

1 tbsp (7.5 g) chipotle chile powder

¼ tsp ground cumin

1 tbsp (3 g) dried oregano

1 cup (235 ml) Herbed Chicken Stock (page 166), or store-bought

3½ lb (1.6 kg) pork shoulder, skin off, cut into 3" (7.5-cm) pieces

Place all of the ingredients except the pork in a large mixing bowl and mix well with a spoon or spatula. Using tongs, place the pork in the pressure cooker. Ladle all of the sauce over the pork. Do not stir. Close the lid.

Stovetop: Set to high pressure (15 PSI) and cook over high heat for 35 minutes total. When the pressure has been reached, lower the heat to medium-high and continue to cook.

Electric: Use the meat/poultry setting, or set to high pressure (10–12 PSI) and 45 minutes.

When done, remove from the heat or turn off the cooker and allow the pressure to release on its own (natural-release), 10 to 12 minutes.

When all of the pressure is out, open the lid and skim off any excess fat from the top. Transfer the pork to a carving or cutting board and shred the meat, using tongs or your hands if you're comfortable doing so, and serve.

Irish-Style Corned Beef with Cabbage and Vegetables

I first discovered this dish in downtown Washington, D.C., at a hot buffet bar directly across the street from the White House. It was always the first dish to run out during lunch. It's great not having to wait for a great dish when you have a simple recipe to follow. Mine is beautifully aromatic and enjoyable much faster. Also, I think you should try making this with your favorite stout beer for added caramelization and flavor!

SERVES 4 TO 6

2½ lb (1.1 kg) corned beef (without the seasoning packet)

4½ cups (1.1 L) water or Herbed Beef Stock (page 167), or store-bought (see tip)

3 bay leaves

3 whole allspice berries

6 juniper berries

4 whole cloves

2 cloves garlic, peeled, left whole

½ tsp black peppercorns

⅛ tsp mustard powder

½ tsp coriander seeds

4 sprigs thyme

12 oz (355 ml) amber or stout beer (optional; see tip)

1 tsp (6 g) kosher salt

4 carrots, sliced diagonally in 1½" (4-cm) pieces

4 cups (440 g) baby potato medley, or 4 medium red potatoes, skin on, quartered

1 small head savoy cabbage, quartered into wedges

Add the corned beef, water or stock, all of the spices and herbs and the beer, if using (see tip), to the pressure cooker. Season with the salt and close the lid.

Stovetop: Set to high pressure (15 PSI) and cook over high heat for 50 minutes.

Electric: Use the meat/poultry setting, or set to high pressure (10–12 PSI) and 60 minutes.

When done, remove from the heat or cancel cooking and release the pressure, using auto-release. Open the cooker and remove the beef, using tongs. Reserve the pot juice. Transfer the beef to a carving board and cover with aluminum foil. Allow it to rest, about 5 minutes. While the beef is resting, make the vegetable medley: Add all of the vegetables to the cooker with the remaining pot juice and stir. Close the lid.

Stovetop: Set to high pressure (15 PSI) and cook over high heat for 4 minutes total.

Electric: Set to high pressure (10–12 PSI) and 6 minutes.

When done, remove from the heat or turn off the cooker and allow the pressure to release on its own (natural-release) for 10 minutes, then apply auto-release. When all of the pressure is out, open the lid and strain the vegetables, discarding all of the spices and herbs. Adjust for salt. Slice the corned beef, lengthwise, to your desired thickness, generally about 1½ inches (4 cm). To plate, distribute the corned beef and vegetables on each plate.

B'S COOKING TIP: You can use an amber or stout beer in lieu of part of the water. If so, reduce the water amount by 1½ cups (355 ml) and add the entire 12-ounce (355-ml) can of beer. The alcohol will burn off but the color and flavor are set in well.

YOUR NEW FAVORITE BEEF TONGUE DISH

Lengua de Res

If you've never had beef tongue, I'm honored to introduce you to it. It is by far the tenderest cut of meat I've ever eaten. And I've eaten plenty. When cooked properly, it is beefy butter heaven. It is tender and juicy, two attributes that make beef so favored. I've been eating *lengua* since I was a young child in Miami, but my mother didn't make it as much as I would have loved. This delicate cut is complemented by a robust tomato and red wine sauce that will leave you swooning. Something to note, however, is that peeling the skin is a task worthy of patience. I learned how to make tongue in the pressure cooker with the skin on, taking about one hour. Skinning it before cooking reduces the cooking time by fifteen or so minutes, but requires confident knife skills. This recipe is for the eager cook wanting to practice cooking virtues. If you don't want to bother with skinning, your butcher will be happy to do it for you when you buy the tongue.

SERVES 4 TO 6

2 lb (905 g) beef tongue

1 tsp (6 g) kosher salt

6 cloves garlic, minced

2 tbsp (28 ml) canola oil

1 medium Spanish onion, sliced

1 orange bell pepper, julienned

1 large bay leaf

½ tsp ground cumin

1 tsp (1 g) dried oregano

¼ tsp red pepper flakes

2 tbsp (28 ml) white distilled vinegar

½ cup (123 g) tomato sauce

1½ cups (355 ml) medium-bodied red wine

1½ cups (355 ml) Herbed Beef Stock (page 167), or store-bought

Clean the tongue really well, even scrubbing with a kitchen brush if your hands don't do the job. Remove the top layer of the skin and any excess fat with a paring knife or a sharp chef's knife. Cut a slit at the tip and score down about 2 inches (5 cm). Put some heart into it and start pulling back the skin. Rub down the whole tongue with salt and garlic. Slice it crosswise into 2-inch (5-cm) cutlets.

Heat the oil over medium for the stovetop pressure cooker or use the sauté function for the electric pressure cooker. Lightly sauté the onion and bell pepper, about 2 to 4 minutes.

Transfer the tongue, including the seasonings, to the cooker. Add the bay leaf, cumin, oregano, red pepper flakes, vinegar and tomato sauce, in that order. Using a wooden spoon, stir well to combine all of the ingredients, maintaining on medium heat or the sauté function for 2 more minutes. Pour in the red wine and beef stock. Stir, cancel cooking for the electric cooker and close the lid.

Stovetop: Set to high pressure (15 PSI) and set your timer for 35 minutes. Cook over high heat. With 10 minutes remaining, reduce the heat to medium and continue to cook.

Electric: Use the bean setting, or set to high pressure (10–12 PSI) and 40 minutes.

When done, remove from the heat or turn off the cooker and release the pressure, using auto-release. When all of the pressure is out, open the lid and let the meat rest for a few minutes while in the pressure cooker. Adjust for salt. Transfer the tongue to a serving platter, using tongs. Ladle the gravy all over the tongue. Be ready for some serious goodness.

(continued)

This robust beef is so dense and rich in flavor, it doesn't need much else to enjoy. I've always loved it best with white rice. It allows you to simply savor the meat. Ladle a generous amount of gravy to saturate the rice. A bright green salad with figs, cheese, fennel and cherry tomato is a good accompaniment.

B'S COOKING TIP: Reserve and store all of the skin for later to make a fatty and really flavorful stock.

B IN THE KNOW! Beef tongue can take up to 2 hours to cook conventionally. While pressure cooking may slightly shrink the size of your cuts, the high temperatures and high level of retained moisture allow for this delicate cut to stay juicy. The loss of collagen turns into gelatin, which makes well-done meats succulent and tender. This particular dish should be supertender and almost too easy to cut with your knife.

Global Tastebuds 🌐

Many cultures around the world have been enjoying the buttery delicacy of beef tongue in varied styles for centuries. Ironically, with the plethora of abundant resources Americans boast, we've not sung its praises until recently. It's now considered quasi- "haute" cuisine with gourmet chefs putting a fancy spin on it. Here are some common ways a few countries enjoy tongue. Have fun experimenting in your own way.

Mexico: Braised and almost overcooked tongue is wildly popular in tacos.

Russia: A very popular but expensive cut served in restaurants. Traditionally cooked in white sauce. It's also added to leafy salads.

England: Brits usually use ox tongue, and pressed with gelatin for the old-fashioned cold dish of pressed tongue.

Vietnam: Thinly sliced and used in pho (see my recipe on page 159).

Middle East: Depending on the country, it can be enjoyed in stews, shredded and added to salads, and formed into meatballs.

Hearty Beef with Rustic Potatoes

Carne con Papa

I considered adding this recipe to the "Classic and Fusion Plates from My Cuban Kitchen" chapter, since it's inspired by one of the first dishes I learned how to cook. The base for the sauce was much simpler then. My version now is a notch up with color and flavor from the rosemary, something not seen or used often in Cuba until more recently. This dish is so well rounded you may find yourself enjoying it over pasta, simple white rice (yes, a starch on starch faux pas!) or paired with roasted vegetables. One thing I love to do with meats, especially classic Cuban dishes, is to add a detectable yet subtle pinch of nutmeg, or even allspice, but not both. This is a good recipe to try out one or the other if you want to add a bit of an aromatic. Try it! It's spectacular.

Serves 4 to 6

2½ lb (1.1 kg) top round, trimmed of fat, cut into 2" (5-cm) pieces

1½ tsp (9 g) kosher salt

1 cup diced yellow onion

1 red bell pepper, julienned

6 cloves garlic, mashed and minced

1 tsp (2.5) ground cumin

1 heaping tsp (1.5 g) dried oregano

3 sprigs rosemary

2 tbsp (28 ml) white distilled vinegar

1 cup (245 g) tomato sauce

2 cups (475 ml) dry cooking wine

¼ cup (60 ml) canola oil

1 tsp (3 g) capers, rinsed

1 cup (235 ml) Herbed Beef Stock (page 167), or store-bought

2 medium russet potatoes, peeled and cut into 1½" (4-cm) pieces

Freshly ground black pepper

Add the beef, salt, onion, bell pepper, garlic, cumin, oregano, rosemary and vinegar to the pressure cooker. Mix well, combining all of the ingredients. Pour in the tomato sauce, cooking wine, oil, capers and beef stock. Stir and close the lid.

Stovetop: Set to high pressure (15 PSI) and cook over high heat for 30 minutes total.

Electric: Set to high pressure (10–12 PSI) and 35 minutes.

When done, remove from the heat or cancel cooking and release the pressure, using auto-release. When all of the pressure is out, open the lid and add the potatoes. Adjust for salt and pepper and gently stir, using a wooden spoon. Close the lid.

Stovetop: Set to high pressure (15 PSI) and cook for 8 to 10 minutes over medium-high heat.

Electric: Set to high pressure (10–12 PSI) and 15 minutes.

When done, remove from the heat or turn off the cooker and allow the pressure to release on its own (natural-release) for 7 to 10 minutes, then turn the valve to auto-release to finish releasing the pressure. Open the lid and remove the rosemary sprigs.

B'S COOKING TIP: This dish is equally delicious with creamy mashed potatoes. Simply omit the potatoes in this recipe and reduce the sauce for 10 minutes when done cooking under pressure.

MEXICAN CHIPOTLE CARNITAS

This equally simple meat dish is flavored a bit like the Braised Pulled Pork BBQ on page 48, but the key difference is that the sauce is well-absorbed into the meat, making it ideal for tacos, open-faced tortilla "tacos" or your favorite style of fajita.

SERVES 4

1 tbsp (15 ml) canola oil

1¼ lb (567 g) pork shoulder, cut into 1½" (4-cm) cubes

1 cup (160 g) finely chopped Spanish onion

½ cup (75 g) finely chopped red bell pepper

1 tbsp (10 g) finely chopped garlic

1½ tbsp (11 g) chipotle chile powder

¼ tsp ground thyme

1 tbsp (3 g) dried oregano

¼ tsp ground cumin

¾ tbsp (4.5 g) kosher salt

½ tsp freshly ground black pepper

1 cup (180 g) crushed tomatoes

1½ cups (355 ml) Herbed Chicken Stock (page 166), or store-bought

2 small bay leaves

Heat the canola oil in the pressure cooker over high for the stovetop pressure cooker or use the browning setting for the electric pressure cooker. Add the pork and brown on all sides, turning with tongs, about 3 to 4 minutes.

Add the onion, pepper and garlic and sauté for 2 to 3 minutes. Cancel cooking for the electric cooker; the residual heat will sauté the vegetables. Add all of the dried spices and herbs, except the bay leaves, and stir. Pour in the crushed tomatoes and chicken stock and stir to blend well all of the ingredients. Add the bay leaves and close the lid.

Stovetop: Set to high pressure (15 PSI) and cook over high heat for 25 minutes total.

Electric: Use the meat/poultry setting, or set to high pressure (10–12 PSI) and 25–30 minutes.

When done, remove from the heat or turn off the cooker and release the pressure, using auto-release. Serve immediately.

Enjoy a taste of Mexico!

Tarragon-Mustard Braised Short Ribs

Mustard and tarragon are a natural couple born in the central region of France. I found a little jar of this sweet pungency during one of my domestic food–based trips. The idea of marinating short ribs with it transported me to Dijon, France, home of the tangy spread. Pair this with additional vegetables such as an herbal chickpea salad or French green beans and a glass of red wine.

Serves 4

2½ lb (1.1 kg) bone-in beef short ribs

1¼ tsp (7.5 g) kosher salt

½ tsp freshly ground black pepper

2 tbsp (28 ml) olive oil

1½ tsp (7.5 g) raw sugar

⅓ cup (58 g) tarragon mustard

3 sprigs fresh thyme, or ½ tsp dried

½ shallot, thinly sliced

4 cloves garlic, mashed

1 cup (235 ml) Herbed Beef Stock (page 176), or store-bought

⅓ cup (80 ml) Merlot

1½ cups (165 g) baby potato medly (red, purple and white), skin on, left whole or cut in half

4 oz (115 g) mushrooms, stemmed and sliced

4 leaves fresh tarragon, thinly sliced, or ½ tsp dried

Season the short ribs with 1 teaspoon (6 g) of the salt and the pepper. Heat the olive oil in the stovetop pressure cooker over high or use the sauté function for the electric pressure cooker. Using tongs, place the short ribs in the cooker and cover with the sugar. For stovetop cookers, lower the heat to medium. Brown the short ribs, about 3 to 5 minutes.

In a small bowl, mix the tarragon mustard and thyme until well blended. Add the shallot and garlic. Using a rubber spatula, cover the short ribs with the mustard sauce. Pour in the beef stock and wine. Add the potatoes, mushrooms and fresh tarragon and season with the remaining ¼ teaspoon of salt. Stir gently, using a wooden spoon. Cancel cooking for the electric cooker, and close the lid.

Stovetop: Set to high pressure (15 PSI) and cook over high heat for 25 minutes total.

Electric: Set to high pressure (10–12 PSI) and 30 minutes.

When done, remove from the heat or turn off the cooker and allow the pressure to release on its own (natural-release), about 10 minutes.

Using tongs, remove the ribs from the cooker and transfer to a serving platter. Allow them to rest for a few minutes before ladling the pot *jus* all over. Garnish with additional tarragon leaves, if desired.

B CREATIVE! If you can't find a jar of tarragon mustard at your local gourmet food store, make your own small batch. Combine ⅓ cup (58 g) of whole-grain Dijon mustard, 3 tablespoons (45 ml) of honey, 1 tablespoon (2 g) of dried tarragon, 1 tablespoon (5 g) of minced fresh tarragon and a pinch of salt.

Spicy Ancho Chile and Cilantro Short Ribs

I used to write a food column for Dean & DeLuca where my job was to play around with a lot of their newest and trendiest ingredients and then develop recipes with the bounty. Of all the recipes I created, this is one of my favorites. The ancho chile powder adds a remarkable smokiness, while the cilantro beautifully brightens it up. Choose the best-quality short ribs you can find. It makes a nice difference in flavor and fat content. Pair with Everyday Sweet Corn Purée (page 178).

SERVES 4

3 lb (1.4 kg) bone-in beef short ribs

1 tsp (6 g) kosher salt

Freshly ground black pepper

½ tsp ground cumin

1 tbsp (7.5 g) ancho chile powder

2 tbsp (28 ml) basil garlic olive oil

3 cloves garlic, chopped

½ cup (8 g) chopped fresh cilantro

1 tsp (3 g) seeded and minced jalapeño pepper

1 cup (235 ml) Simple Vegetable Broth (page 157), or store-bought

¼ cup (60 g) dark brown sugar

1 tbsp (5 g) four-peppercorn blend, crushed

½ cup (120 ml) Herbed Beef Stock (page 167), or store-bought

1 cup (235 ml) red wine (I recommend a good Chilean variety)

Rinse and pat dry the short ribs. Season with the salt, pepper, cumin and ancho chile powder. Heat the olive oil over high for the stovetop pressure cooker or use the browning setting for the electric pressure cooker.

Add the short ribs and brown on all sides, about 4 minutes. While the ribs are browning, make the sauce: Add the garlic, cilantro, jalapeño, vegetable broth, sugar and four-peppercorn blend to a food processor and blend for 1 minute, or until the cilantro has liquefied. Cover the ribs with the mixture, using a rubber spatula to scrape the processor. Pour in the beef stock and wine and stir. Cancel cooking for the electric cooker, and close the lid.

Stovetop: Set to high pressure (15 PSI) and set the timer for 35 minutes. Cook over high heat for 25 minutes, then reduce the heat to medium and continue to cook for the last 10 minutes.

Electric: Set to high pressure (10–12 PSI) and 40 minutes.

When done, remove from the heat or turn off the cooker and allow the pressure to release on its own (natural-release), about 12 minutes.

When all of the pressure is out, adjust for salt and remove the short ribs from the pot. Transfer to a serving platter. Cross-cut across several bones and into three parts or however many bones your ribs have.

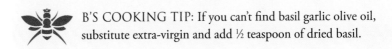 B'S COOKING TIP: If you can't find basil garlic olive oil, substitute extra-virgin and add ½ teaspoon of dried basil.

GUAVA-STUFFED MEATBALLS WITH MINTED BRANDY SAUCE

This decadent sauce was the result of a conversation with my mother about *guayaba* (guava) in Cuba. It is a quasi-bitter tropical fruit that finds its way into sauces, pastries, juices and ice cream all throughout Latin America. Guava paste is much like quince paste, but sweeter, so it's equally enjoyable with a hard cheese, such as Manchego. For a rustically elegant and surprising dish, make these sweet and savory meatballs. You can find guava paste in a round tin cylinder or a rectangular package in either the international or Latin aisle of your local grocery store or market; or you can find it online, too.

YIELD: 24 MEATBALLS

1 lb (455 g) ground chuck beef

1 medium or large egg

½ cup (120 ml) milk

1 cup (115 g) unseasoned bread crumbs

½ Spanish onion, chopped

4 cloves garlic

1 tsp (1 g) red pepper flakes

½ tsp ground cumin

1 tsp (6 g) salt

1 (21-oz [595-g]) can guava paste, at room temperature, cubed, divided

2 tbsp (28 ml) canola oil

1 cup (235 ml) Herbed Beef Stock (page 167), or store-bought

½ cup (120 ml) brandy

½ cup (120 ml) freshly squeezed orange juice, without pulp

1 tsp (5 ml) red wine vinegar

1 cup (60 g) finely chopped fresh mint, plus 2 sprigs for garnish

In a large mixing bowl, combine the beef, egg, milk and bread crumbs. Using bare hands, bind all of the ingredients until the bread crumbs and egg are well incorporated into the beef. Set aside and cover. Place the onion and garlic in a food processor and pulse until both are finely chopped. If you don't have a food processor, finely mince the garlic and cut the onion into a small dice. Add the onion, garlic, red pepper flakes, cumin and salt to the beef and mix well until all of the ingredients are combined. Take a golf ball–size scoop of the beef and make a 3- to 4-inch (7.5- to 10-cm) flat patty in the palm of your hand, creating a divot in the center. Place 1 teaspoon (5 g) of guava in the center and gently round the beef into 2-inch (5-cm) balls. Place and separate them on a cookie sheet while you are making them.

Heat the oil in the stovetop pressure cooker over medium-high or use the sauté function for the electric pressure cooker. Lightly brown the meatballs, stirring gently, about 2 minutes. Add the beef broth, brandy, orange juice and vinegar. Add the remaining guava and the cup (60 g) of fresh mint. Stir to combine all of the ingredients. Cancel cooking for the electric cooker, and close the lid.

Stovetop: Set to high pressure (15 PSI) and cook over high heat for 10 minutes total.

Electric: Use the stew setting, or set to high pressure (10–12 PSI) and 10 minutes.

When done, remove from the heat or turn off the cooker and allow the pressure to release on its own (natural-release), 5 to 7 minutes. Stir and adjust for salt. Transfer the meatballs to your serving platter, using a large slotted spoon. Ladle the sauce over the meatballs. Garnish with fresh mint leaves, chopped or whole.

 B'S COOKING TIP: You can opt out of stuffing the meatballs with guava and reserve it all for the sauce.

Island Oxtails, Yuca and Swiss Chard

I learned an unexpected amount of food culture while writing this book. One little accidental sidebar conversation was about Swiss chard. I had no idea green and rainbow chard were often used in Cuban cuisine. I had even less knowledge that my mother used to feed it to us as children! It's used in a few other classic stews such as *potaje de judías blanca*, a white navy bean stew. This revelation justified the experiments I've taken on since. Combining it with oxtails and yuca was a trio inspired by the popularity each has on its own. Juicy oxtails and starchy yuca are countered with a sweetly bitter green. It instantly became a favorite dinner option around our home.

Serves 4 to 6

2 lb (905 g) oxtails

1 tbsp (18 g) kosher salt, plus more to taste

1 tsp (6 g) garlic salt

½ tsp red pepper flakes

2 tbsp (28 ml) olive oil

1 tsp (1 g) dried oregano

1 bay leaf

1 Vidalia onion, sliced

4 cloves garlic, thinly sliced

2 cups (473 ml) Herbed Beef Stock (page 167), or store-bought

1½ lb (680 g) frozen yuca, cut in half, crosswise

2 bunches or 10 large stalks rainbow Swiss chard, stemmed and cut in half (reserve and julienne 5 stems for garnish)

Season the oxtails with the kosher and garlic salts and the red pepper flakes. Heat the olive oil in the stovetop pressure cooker over medium-high or use the brown function for the electric pressure cooker. Add the oxtails and dried spices and herbs and brown on all sides, about 3 minutes. Add the onion and garlic. Pour the beef broth over the oxtails. Give it a good stir and cook for 2 to 4 minutes. Cancel cooking for the electric cooker, and close the lid.

Stovetop: Set to high pressure (15 PSI) and cook over high heat for 25 minutes total.

Electric: Set to high pressure (10–12 PSI) and 30 minutes.

While the oxtails are cooking in the pressure cooker, cook the yuca in a separate pot on the stove. Add enough water to cover the yuca. Season with salt to taste and gently stir. Cook over medium-high heat for 25 minutes, or until the yuca is mostly tender but not mushy. Strain and set aside.

When the oxtails are done, turn off the heat but keep the stovetop cooker on the range or cancel cooking for the electric cooker. Allow the pressure to release on its own (natural-release). If the pressure is not fully released after 10 minutes, apply auto-release. When all of the pressure is out, add the yuca and the Swiss chard. Cover the cooker but don't apply any pressure. For the stovetop cooker, cook over medium heat for 7 minutes; for the electric cooker, reset to the sauté function and 9 to 10 minutes; or cook until chard is tender but not wilted.

Evenly distribute into individual bowls. Garnish each serving with a handful of julienned Swiss chard stems.

Aromatic and Bright Orange Ginger Chicken

Chicken is often cooked very simply, but there are so many fantastic ways to play with every piece of the bird. Thighs are my favorite piece for their juiciness. The herbal aromas and brightness in this dish prove that chicken is a wonderful base for infusing unique flavors. You can make this a bit more savory by adding one additional teaspoon (5 ml) of soy sauce. As a slight variation, I love lightly charring some of the oranges. It makes the dish pop both in taste and visual appeal in a new way.

Serves 6 to 8

8 chicken thighs, skin on half

7 cloves garlic

1 tbsp (18 g) sea salt

1 tsp (2 g) whole coriander seeds

1 tsp (2.5 g) dried cumin

½ tsp freshly ground black pepper

2 navel oranges, cut into wedges

¼ cup (60 ml) canola or vegetable oil

1 bay leaf

1 tbsp (8 g) grated fresh ginger

4 whole cloves

½ cup (120 ml) dry white wine

1 tbsp (15 ml) low-sodium soy sauce

Few sprigs cilantro, for garnish

Place the chicken on a large baking sheet. Add the garlic to a mortar and mash, using the pestle. Add the salt, coriander, cumin and pepper. Grind and stir with the pestle until the garlic and dried spices are well-blended. Rub all of the chicken with the garlic mixture, covering every piece of chicken very generously. Squeeze 2 orange wedges all over the chicken. If you have time, cover and chill for 30 minutes, to allow all of the flavors to marinate well. Otherwise continue cooking.

Heat the oil in the stovetop pressure cooker over medium-high or use the browning setting for the electric pressure cooker. Transfer the chicken to the cooker, using tongs. Brown on all sides until all of the pieces are lightly golden, about 4 minutes. If your cooker is small or narrow, do this in two batches. Add the bay leaf, ginger, cloves, white wine and 2 or 3 additional orange wedges, giving them a hard squeeze. Cancel cooking for the electric cooker, and close the lid.

Stovetop: Set to high pressure (15 PSI) and set your timer for 17 minutes total. Cook on high heat until the pressure point is reached, then reduce the heat to medium to finish cooking.

Electric: Set to high pressure (10–12 PSI) and 20–22 minutes.

When done, remove from the heat or turn off the cooker and release the pressure, using auto-release. When all of the pressure is out, transfer the chicken to your serving platter, leaving the pot juice in the cooker. Discard the orange wedges from the cooker. Stir in the soy sauce. Bring the pot juice to a boil, then lower the heat to a simmer, about 5 minutes, allowing the sauce to reduce just a bit. Ladle the sauce over the chicken and garnish with fresh cilantro sprigs and the remaining orange wedges.

OLD-SCHOOL, NEW-SCHOOL POACHED CUBAN-STYLE MEAT LOAF

This meat loaf was my mother's bright idea and I couldn't be more pleased to share it with you. I modified it to fit my palate and also to introduce her to ingredients unfamiliar to her. The result was a fusion of Cuban technique and American staples.

SERVES 4 TO 6

1 lb (455 g) ground beef

1 lb (455 g) ground pork

5 cloves garlic, finely minced

1 tbsp (18 g) smoked salt

2 tsp (1 g) dried parsley

1 tsp (2 g) freshly grated nutmeg

½ tsp freshly ground black pepper

½ tsp ground cumin

¾ cup (175 ml) milk

4 medium or large eggs

1 tbsp (11 g) brown mustard

2 cups (475 ml) water or Herbed Beef Stock (page 167), or store-bought

1 yellow onion, sliced

1 bay leaf

1 tsp (1 g) dried oregano

1 tbsp (15 ml) plus 1 tsp (5 ml) Worcestershire sauce

½ cup (120 g) ketchup

1 tsp (5 ml) soy sauce

Preheat the oven to 450°F (230°C). In a large mixing bowl, combine the ground beef and pork, garlic and all of the dried seasonings, except the bay leaf and oregano. Using your hands, blend well. Add the milk, eggs and mustard. Use your hands again or a flat wooden spoon to incorporate all of the ingredients. Set aside. Add the water or beef stock, onion, bay leaf and oregano to the pressure cooker. Bring to a light boil over medium heat for the stovetop cooker, or use the sauté setting for the electric cooker, about 3 to 4 minutes. While the onion cooks, transfer the meat to a large baking sheet. Mold the meat into your desired size. I recommend 2 inches (5 cm) in height and 5–5½ inches (12–14 cm) wide. Use the back of a wooden spoon to flatten the edges. Douse 1 tablespoon (15 ml) of the Worcestershire over top of the loaf. Dampen a superthin kitchen towel or cheesecloth and wrap the loaf in the cloth. Gently tie with twine to secure the cloth. Gently place the loaf in the pressure cooker. Cancel cooking for the electric cooker, and close the lid.

Stovetop: Set to high pressure (15 PSI) and cook over high heat for 15 minutes total.

Electric: Set to high pressure (10–12 PSI) and 15 minutes.

When done, remove from the heat or turn off the cooker and allow the pressure to release on its own (natural-release), about 10 minutes. If the pressure is not fully released after 10 minutes, apply auto-release. Reduce the oven heat to 350°F (180°C). When you can handle the heat, remove the loaf from the cooker. Drain the water, reserving the onions, and remove the cheesecloth. Place the loaf on a clean baking sheet. In a small mixing bowl, blend the cooked onions, ketchup, soy sauce and remaining teaspoon (5 ml) of Worcestershire. Spread the mixture all over the loaf, covering the sides. Bake for 15 minutes, or until the glaze has caramelized. Enjoy this with a garlicky bed of spinach or the Vibrant Yellow Vegetable Rice on page 93.

 B'S COOKING TIP: If your oven has a broiler, preheat while the loaf is cooking. Add the loaf to the broiler for a few minutes, or until the glaze has caramelized.

Fig and Syrah Lamb Shanks

I have a childhood friend whose mother has a healthy fig tree but doesn't like them at all. However, it works really well for me. When in season, he drops off baskets filled with black Mission figs. I eat them as snacks, chop them up for salads, slice them and pour Madeira balsamic vinegar over them and enjoy with cheese. The list goes on. For bigger dishes, they work well to add sweetness and texture. I love how they work with these lovely shanks. This is an exquisite option for family dinners or impressing your guests during the holidays.

Serves 6 to 8

4 lbs (1.8 kg) bone-in lamb shanks

7 cloves garlic, mashed

1 tbsp (18 g) kosher salt

2 tsp (1 g) ground dried sage

¼ cup (60 ml) plus 1 tbsp (15 ml) extra-virgin olive oil

1½ cups (355 ml) Syrah wine

1½ cups (355 ml) Herbed Beef Stock (page 167), or store-bought

12 sprigs thyme

3 bay leaves

4 shallots, thinly sliced

3 carrots, cut into 1" (2.5 cm) slices

1 handful dried black Mission figs, left whole

1 tsp (2 g) freshly ground black pepper

Salt to taste

Fresh sage leaves, for garnish

Rinse and pat dry the shanks. Place them on a parchment paper–lined baking sheet. In a medium wooden or marble mortar, add the garlic, 1½ teaspoons (9 g) of the salt, the sage and the tablespoon (15 ml) of olive oil. Mash, using the pestle, until you have a semithick paste. Rub the seasoning mixture all over the shanks, covering them fully. If you have time, cover them with aluminum foil and chill for 1 hour.

Heat the stovetop pressure cooker over high or use the browning setting for the electric pressure cooker. Add the remaining ¼ cup (60 ml) of olive oil. Using large tongs, place the lamb shanks in the cooker and brown, turning once, about 4 to 5 minutes total.

Pour in the wine and beef stock and add the thyme, bay leaves, shallots and carrots. Reduce the heat to low for the stovetop pressure cooker or cancel the browning function on the electric pressure cooker and reset to the simmer setting, and cook for 5 minutes. Add the figs and pepper and season with salt to taste. If you can, stir very gently, using a small-headed wooden spoon. Cancel cooking for the electric cooker, and close the lid.

Stovetop: Set to high pressure (15 PSI) and set the timer for 30 minutes. Cook over high heat until the pressure point is reached, about 15 minutes, then turn down the heat to medium and continue to cook for the remaining 15 minutes.

Electric: Set to high pressure (10–12 PSI) and 35 minutes.

When done, remove from the heat or turn off the cooker and allow the pressure to release on its own (natural-release), about 10 minutes. If the pressure is not fully released after 10 minutes, apply auto-release. If you'd like to reduce the sauce, remove the shanks and cook over medium heat for 6 to 10 minutes for the stovetop cooker or use the simmer or sauté function for the electric cooker, or until desired consistency is reached.

Using tongs, remove the shanks and arrange on your serving platter or on individual plates. Ladle the sauce all over. Garnish with fresh sage.

SUPERFAST BEANS, LEGUMES AND PEAS

Beans are the staple and base of food for many underdeveloped countries. Rice harvests and relatively inexpensive bulk rates for beans relegated them to being the default dinner in many homes. I grew up eating beans—about ten different varieties—and other legumes almost daily. If it weren't for the superquick cooking time the pressure cooker allows for hard grains and stubborn beans, I'm sure my diet would have been significantly different. Overnight soaking and three- to four-hour conventional cook times are now 45 minutes, tops, in your pressure cooker. That attractive time savings invites a myriad of foods and dishes you can explore and incorporate into your growing recipe files. If making chickpeas in just one hour isn't enticing enough, how about risotto in eleven minutes? It's splendid and amazing at the same time. These recipes are a combination of classic dishes I enjoyed as a child and dishes I've developed over the years. This small collection is a mustard-seed size idea of what you can accomplish in the pressure cooker. It goes without saying, I'm particularly fond of the Famous Cuban Black Beans (page 72) in this collection. Read on and enjoy a true part of Cuban culture.

FAMOUS CUBAN BLACK BEANS

Black beans are Cuba's most beloved food. They are pedestaled to glorious heights in Cuban homes around the world. You've seen and probably made a version of these "Cuban black beans" at some point in your Latin food exploits, but you've never made *these*. This is my late grandmother's recipe as translated and perfected by my mother for over 40 years. Her beans are the point of query after reconnecting with childhood friends. They are the single food in my family that is still rationed. It's the one dish that humbles my skill. I can make my mother's beans, side by side with her, but hers will always exceed triumph. There's something indiscernibly magical about her touch. I hold this recipe close to my heart, but have waited for over a decade to share it publicly. I hope you love them as much as everyone who's ever eaten in Mami's *cocina*. For your convenience and ease, this recipe does not require any soaking.

Goya and Rancho Gordo dried beans are my go-to brands. To enjoy a very classic experience, ladle about one cup (172 g) of black beans over fluffy white rice and serve with a side of sweet fried plantains.

SERVES 8 TO 10

3 tbsp (46 ml) canola oil

½ Spanish onion, diced

½ green bell pepper, diced

4 cloves garlic, minced

1 tsp (1 g) dried oregano

½ tsp ground cumin

16 oz (455 g) dried black beans, picked over and rinsed

2 quarts (1.9 L) water or Simple Vegetable Broth (page 157)

2 bay leaves

3 whole cloves

2 tbsp (30 g) raw sugar

1½ tbsp (27 g) kosher salt

1 tsp (5 ml) dry cooking wine

1 tsp (5 ml) olive oil

Heat the oil in the stovetop pressure cooker over high or use the sauté setting for the electric pressure cooker. Make the *sofrito*: Sauté all of the vegetables and garlic, with the oregano and cumin, until it is fragrant and the onion is translucent, about 4 minutes. Reduce the heat to low or cancel the sauté setting. Add all of the remaining ingredients, except the cooking wine and olive oil, to the cooker and stir to combine well. Close the lid.

Stovetop: Set to high pressure (15 PSI) and set the timer for 35 minutes. Cook over high heat. When the pressure point is reached, reduce the heat to medium and continue to cook.

Electric: Set to high pressure (10–12 PSI) and 40 minutes.

When done, remove from the heat or turn off the cooker and allow the pressure to release on its own (natural-release) for 10 minutes, then apply auto-release. When all of the pressure is out, open the lid and top the beans with the cooking wine and drizzle in the olive oil. Allow the beans to rest a few minutes before serving.

B'S COOKING TIP: If you soak the beans overnight, you can save up to 20 minutes with this recipe! Simply reduce your cooking time by 10–13 minutes. Also, these beans can last up to 1 week in the refrigerator and 4 months in the freezer.

EARTHY CURRIED POTATO LENTILS

My mother doesn't like curry. I love it. She doesn't like lentils. I love them. She loves potatoes. I'm not their biggest fan. But together, our joint effort in making food for the soul harmoniously results in something we both can enjoy. These curried lentils are thick enough on their own but simple enough to pair with a juicy steak or over basmati rice. The curry and potato combination is a pigeonhole view into everyday Indian flavors, one of my favorite cuisines.

SERVES 6 TO 8

2 tbsp (28 ml) olive oil

1 cup (160 g) diced yellow onion

5 cloves garlic, minced

1 tsp (2 g) cumin seeds

¼ tsp ground turmeric

2½ quarts (2.4 L) water or Simple Vegetable Broth (page 157)

4 tsp (8 g) curry powder

3 white potatoes, peeled and cubed in 1½" (4-cm) pieces

1 cup (130 g) sliced carrot (small slices)

16 oz (455 g) dried lentils

1 large bay leaf

1 tbsp (18 g) kosher salt

Freshly ground black pepper

Fresh flat-leaf parsley, for garnish (optional)

Heat the olive oil in the stovetop pressure cooker over high or use the sauté setting for the electric pressure cooker. Sauté the onion and garlic until the onion is translucent, about 2 minutes. Season with the cumin seeds and turmeric. Reduce the heat for the stovetop cooker, or cancel cooking and reset to the simmer setting for the electric cooker. Stir in the water or vegetable broth and the curry powder. Bring to a light boil. Add the potatoes, carrot, lentils and bay leaf. Season with salt and black pepper. Cancel cooking for the electric cooker, and close the lid.

Stovetop: Set to high pressure (15 PSI) and cook over high heat for 20 minutes total.

Electric: Set to high pressure (10–12 PSI) and 25 minutes.

When done, remove from the heat or turn off the cooker and allow the pressure to release on its own (natural-release). When all of the pressure is out, open the cooker and stir gently, using a wooden spoon. Adjust for salt.

Garnish individual servings with parsley, if desired.

 B'S COOKING TIP: If you prefer a bit thicker consistency, cook uncovered for 5 minutes over medium heat or using the simmer function. For a more soupy consistency, add 1 additional cup (235 ml) of water or broth and simmer for 5 minutes.

PASTA E FAGIOLI

This once peasant dish ubiquitous in Italy is modern enough for us to enjoy on a chilly night. The nice thing is how easily adjustable it is. Switch out the beans and meat for your own favorite. The pasta shape can be changed, too. I love the combo of the medium-sized shells with the pinto, which tend to be on the bigger side. It's wonderful with crusty bread, which soaks up any spare broth.

SERVES 6

1 cup (215 g) dried pinto beans

6 cups (1.4 L) water or Simple Vegetable Broth (page 157)

3 bay leaves

3 tbsp (45 ml) canola oil

4 oz (115 g) or 3 slices applewood-smoked bacon, chopped

1 carrot, diced

1 stalk celery, diced

1 medium white onion, diced

½ yellow bell pepper, diced

2 cloves garlic, minced

2 spring onions, diced

1 tbsp (3 g) dried oregano

1½ tbsp (24 g) tomato paste

1 tsp (1 g) chopped fresh dill

1 cup (93 g) uncooked medium pasta shells

1 tsp (6 g) kosher salt and more to taste

Add the beans, water or vegetable broth, and bay leaves to the pressure cooker. Close the lid.

Stovetop: Set to high pressure (15 PSI) and set the timer for 20 minutes. Cook over high heat until the pressure is reached, then reduce the heat to medium and continue to cook.

Electric: Set to high pressure (10–12 PSI) and 20 minutes.

While the beans are cooking, cook the bacon and vegetables: Heat the oil in a large skillet over medium, add the bacon, carrots and celery and cook until slightly browned, about 3 minutes. Stir in the white onion, bell pepper, garlic and spring onions and season with the oregano. Cook until fragrant, about 2 minutes. Stir in the tomato paste and dill and continue to cook over medium heat, another 2 minutes.

When the beans are done, turn off the heat or cancel cooking and allow the pressure to release on its own (natural-release), about 4 minutes. When all of the pressure is out, open the lid and stir in the bacon and vegetable mixture, the pasta and the salt. Close the lid.

Stovetop: Set to high pressure (15 PSI) and cook over high heat for 10 minutes total.

Electric: Set to high pressure (10–12 PSI) and 10 minutes.

When done, turn off the heat or turn off the cooker and allow the pressure to release on its own (natural-release), about 10 to 12 minutes. If pressure still remains at 12 minutes, turn the valve to the auto-release position. Open the pressure cooker, stir and adjust for salt. Serve immediately.

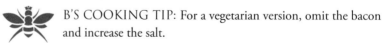 B'S COOKING TIP: For a vegetarian version, omit the bacon and increase the salt.

CHICKPEAS AND KALE

Chickpeas are really a legume but are commonly considered beans. They are the hardest of all the beans I've ever worked with and can take up to 15 percent longer to cook than other dried beans. Their nutritional value is so high, it's worth the time. While they are wildly popular in other parts of the world, the humble chickpea only recently started to gain some attention in America. Hummus is made with chickpeas and more and more salads feature them. I love them in this stewlike pot of kale for their earthy contribution to the greens. A little bit of heat and acid finish it off nicely. The toasted pine nuts complete it. Pour it over couscous and you have a really healthy bowl. You can enjoy this alone, too!

SERVES 6

10 cups (650 g) chopped kale (about 1 large bunch)

1 (16-oz [455-g]) can chickpeas, rinsed and drained

½ cup (80 g) diced white onion

1 (15-oz [425-g]) can whole or Roma tomatoes in sauce (see tip)

1 tsp (5 g) red wine vinegar

3 cloves garlic, minced

1 tbsp (15 ml) olive oil

½ tsp adobo powder

¼ tsp cayenne pepper

⅛ tsp ground cumin

2 tsp dried basil

1 tbsp (18 g) kosher salt, or to taste

⅛ tsp freshly ground black pepper, or to taste

¼ cup (35 g) toasted pine nuts, plus more for garnish (optional)

Fresh basil, for garnish

Rinse and pat dry the kale. Add all of the ingredients, except the pine nuts, to the pressure cooker in the order listed and stir well to combine. Close the lid.

Stovetop: Set to high pressure (15 PSI) and cook over high heat for 5 minutes total.

Electric: Set to high pressure (10–12 PSI) and 6 minutes.

When done, remove from the heat or turn off the cooker and allow the pressure to release on its own (natural-release), about 5 minutes. If the pressure is not fully released after 5 minutes, apply auto-release. When done, add the ¼ cup (35 g) of pine nuts and stir. Adjust for salt and pepper.

Serve with warm couscous and garnish with additional toasted pine nuts and fresh basil.

 B CREATIVE! If preferred as a soup, add ¾ cup (175 ml) of vegetable broth and let simmer for an additional 5 to 10 minutes for the stovetop cooker or using the simmer function for the electric cooker.

 B'S COOKING TIP: Use a can of Roma tomatoes that's already flavored with basil and garlic. If using regular Roma, add more basil and garlic to taste.

Navy Bean and Smoked Turkey Sausage "Chili"

When an elderly friend of my parents in Miami begged me to play around with beans and turkey sausage, I ended up with this beautiful combination of textures and colors. The smoked turkey sausage was the exact meat it needed to make it casual yet elaborate. I interpreted this "new" dish and added cabbage and carrots to make something bright and appealing for dinner. Play around with different beans, too. The layers in this dish can make it a chili, a stew or a mélange.

Serves 6

16 oz (455 g) dried navy beans, picked through and rinsed

2 quarts (1.9 L) Herbed Beef Stock (page 167), or store-bought

1 large bay leaf

¼ cup (60 ml) olive oil

½ yellow onion, diced

1 stalk celery, diced

½ green bell pepper, diced

½ red bell pepper, diced

¼ tsp ground cumin

1 tsp (1 g) dried oregano

13 oz (370 g) smoked turkey sausage, sliced diagonally in 2" (5-cm) pieces

½ cup (123 g) tomato sauce

½ cup (120 ml) white cooking wine

Leaves from 7 sprigs cilantro

1 tsp (2.5 g) jalapeño, seeded and diced (optional)

2 carrots, sliced

2 cups (180 g) chopped cabbage (2" to 3" [5- to 7.5-cm]) pieces

1 tsp (6 g) kosher salt

Add the beans, beef stock and bay leaf to the cooker. Close the lid.

Stovetop: Set to high pressure (15 PSI) and cook over high heat for 40 minutes total. When the pressure point is reached, reduce the heat to medium-high or enough to maintain high pressure and continue to cook.

Electric: Set to high pressure (10–12 PSI) and 40 minutes.

While the beans are cooking, make the turkey sauce: Heat the olive oil in a large skillet over low heat and sauté all of the vegetables except for the carrots and cabbage, adding the cumin and oregano, about 2 minutes. Add the turkey sausage, tomato sauce, cooking wine, cilantro and jalapeño (if desired). Stir, cover and cook over low heat for 10 minutes.

When the beans are done, remove from the heat or cancel the electric cooker and release the pressure, using quick-release for the stovetop cooker or auto-release for the electric cooker. When all of the pressure is out, open the lid and stir in the turkey sauce. Stir in the carrots and cabbage and season with the salt. Close the lid.

Stovetop: Set to high pressure (15 PSI) and cook over high heat for 6 minutes.

Electric: Set to high pressure (10–12 PSI) and 7 minutes.

When done, remove from the heat or turn off the electric cooker and allow the pressure to release on its own (natural-release), about 7 to 10 minutes. If the pressure has not fully released after 10 minutes, apply auto-release. When all of the pressure is out, open the lid and adjust for salt.

B'S COOKING TIP: The consistency of this colorful dish allows you to eat it over rice or certain pasta. Penne, large shells or tubular and circular pastas are best. Another way you can enjoy this is by adding a bit of orzo when you add the carrots and cabbage.

Spicy Lentils with Pulled Flank Steak

I think lentils are the perfect legume to introduce you to making all kinds of legumes, peas and beans in the pressure cooker. They break down pretty fast in the cooker, allowing you to enjoy them as often as you like, and have the added benefit of high levels of vitamins. I added flank steak to this simple pot of brown lentils as a way to give you a one-stop dinner option.

SERVES 4 TO 6

1 lb (455 g) flank steak, trimmed of fat and cut into ½" (1.3-cm) pieces

2 tsp (12 g) kosher salt

½ tsp freshly ground black pepper

3 tbsp (45 ml) vegetable oil

1 Spanish onion, diced

4 cloves garlic, minced

1 tbsp (9 g) seeded and minced jalapeño pepper, plus more if desired

1 tsp (1 g) dried oregano

⅛ tsp ground cumin

1 quart (946 ml) water or Herbed Chicken Stock (page 166)

8 oz (225 g) dried brown lentils 1⅛ c

4 brown or Kumato tomatoes, peeled and quartered

1 tbsp (16 g) tomato paste

1 tsp (5 ml) distilled white vinegar

2 small bay leaves

Season the flank steak with salt and black pepper. Heat the oil in the stovetop pressure cooker over high or use the sauté setting for the electric pressure cooker. Sauté the onion, garlic and jalapeño, seasoning with the oregano and cumin, until very fragrant, about 3 minutes. Add the beef and brown on all sides, over medium-high heat for the stovetop cooker or maintaining the sauté function for the electric cooker, 2 to 4 minutes. Add the water or chicken stock and reduce the heat to medium for the stovetop cooker or cancel the sauté setting for the electric cooker. Add all the remaining ingredients and stir, using a wooden spoon. Close the lid.

Stovetop: Set to high pressure (15 PSI) and cook over high heat for 20 minutes total.

Electric: Set to high pressure (10–12 PSI) and 25 minutes.

When done, turn off the heat or turn off the cooker and allow the pressure to release on its own (natural-release), 8 to 9 minutes. When all of the pressure is out, open the cooker and discard the bay leaves before serving. Adjust for salt. Serve over fluffy white rice.

B'S COOKING TIP: Alternately, you may enjoy the lentils as a hearty soup by adding an additional cup (235 ml) of stock and letting it simmer for 5 minutes, uncovered.

B IN THE KNOW! There are over 10 varieties of lentils to choose from and enjoy. For this recipe, I opted for the more accessible brown lentil, but if you can find it, check out the Beluga, which makes for a luxurious salad. Yellow, dark or light green, petite crimson and the French green are others you can experiment with.

Meaty Brazilian Feijoada

Feijoada is Brazilians' version of a delicious black bean *potaje*, only theirs is heavily stocked with a variety of meats. There are hundreds of variations, some more simple than this one. This elaborate recipe has enough meat to be a meat lover's dream come true. Smoky meats and aromatic spices make it a wonderful option for ambient fall and winter nights.

SERVES 6 TO 8

2 tbsp (28 ml) canola oil

1 yellow onion, chopped

1 red bell pepper, chopped

6 cloves garlic, minced

2 bay leaves

1 cup (60 g) chopped flat-leaf parsley

8 oz (225 g) smoked ham hocks

8 oz (225 g) pork belly, trimmed of skin and cut into 1" (2.5-cm) cubes

8 oz (225 g) Italian sausage, sliced ¼" (6-mm) thick

Salt and freshly ground black pepper

1 tsp (2 g) freshly grated nutmeg

16 oz (455 g) dried black beans, picked over and rinsed

1 quart (946 ml) water

1 cup (235 ml) Herbed Beef Stock (page 167), or store-bought

1 tbsp (15 ml) olive oil

Heat the oil in the stovetop pressure cooker over medium-high or use the sauté setting for the electric pressure cooker. Sauté the onion, bell pepper and garlic until the onion is translucent, about 4 to 6 minutes. Add the bay leaves and parsley and mix well. Add all of the meat and season with the salt, black pepper and nutmeg. Cook until the sausage is browned, about 4 minutes. Add the beans, water and beef stock and stir to blend well all of the ingredients. Cancel cooking for the electric cooker, and close the lid.

Stovetop: Set to high pressure (15 PSI) and set the timer for 45 minutes. Cook over high heat for 25 minutes, or until the pressure point has been reached, then reduce the heat to medium and continue to cook for the remaining 20 minutes.

Electric: Use the bean setting, or set to high pressure (10–12 PSI) and 40 minutes.

When done, turn off the heat or turn off the cooker and allow the pressure to release on its own (natural-release), about 15 minutes. When all of the pressure is out, open the cooker and drizzle in the olive oil. Stir and adjust for salt.

Serve over hot white rice. Also works with brown rice, for a healthier option.

 B'S COOKING TIP: You may enjoy this as a soup. Simply add an additional ½ to 1 cup (120 to 235 ml) of beef stock.

SIMPLE RICE, GRAINS AND PASTA

Just as with beans and peas, I grew up on rice. Today, if I don't feel like cooking an elaborate meal—carb, meat, vegetable—I quickly make a pot of white rice, slice a variety of juicy tomatoes and top my rice with a seductive fried, runny egg. It is simple glory! It is very much a peasant approach to eating but it does the job. Rice is more enjoyable and more inclusive when it's done in half the time of the traditional method in a conventional pot. Your patience will no longer be tested, especially when making brown rice. I also love that these rice and grain dishes are a great source of fiber. Did you ever think cooking rice and fish together could be a brilliant move? Check out the fluffy Herbed Coconut Cod Rice on page 102. I also encourage you try the Black Truffle Cheese Risotto (page 86) and the Decadent 4-Cheese Truffle Mac and Cheese (page 105), two of my favorite recipes in this chapter. The use of fresh truffle or derivatives of the truffle (namely oil and salt) will elevate your senses, expand your palate and inspire you to think outside the box when cooking very traditional foods.

BLACK TRUFFLE CHEESE RISOTTO

Alba, Italy is home to the world's most expensive ingredient: the white truffle. I spent six days there exploring all things related to the elusive fungus, from hunting with a friendly dog to shaving it onto desserts. Risotto is the most perfect bed on which to nestle pungent, paper-thin truffle slices. I had more risotto in that week than I've ever consumed in six months. The experience blew my mind, and I set out to make a more accessible version for us all to enjoy. I wanted to make a really creamy, aromatic and delicious risotto that would mentally take you there and always remind me of that special trip. I like to eat this risotto with the Braised Peppered Red Wine Oxtail (page 112).

SERVES 4 TO 6

1 tbsp (15 ml) olive oil

2 shallots, minced

2 cloves garlic, minced

1 quart (946 ml) chicken broth

½ cup (120 ml) dry white wine

2 tbsp (28 g) unsalted butter

2 tsp (2 g) fresh thyme

1½ cups (293 g) uncooked Arborio rice, washed and rinsed

2½ oz (70 g) goat's milk black truffle cheese

Salt

1 oz (28 g) black truffle, shaved, for garnish (optional)

Roasted asparagus tips, for garnish (optional)

Heat the olive oil in the stovetop pressure cooker over medium-high or use the sauté setting for the electric pressure cooker. Cook the shallots and garlic until the shallots are tender but not browned, about 2 minutes. Add the chicken broth and white wine and stir, using a wooden spoon. Add the butter and thyme and cook over medium heat for the stovetop pressure cooker or cancel the sauté setting for the electric pressure cooker, about 1 minute. Add the rice, stir and close the lid.

Stovetop: Set to high pressure (15 PSI) and cook over high heat for 9 minutes total.

Electric: Set to high pressure (10–12 PSI) and 11 minutes.

When done, remove from the heat or turn off the cooker and allow the pressure to release on its own (natural-release). When all of the pressure is out, open the cooker and gently fold in the truffle cheese, using a large wooden spoon. Adjust for salt, if necessary. Garnish each serving with the shaved black truffle. Alternatively, roasted asparagus tips are a good option also.

B'S COOKING TIP: If you can't find truffle cheese, substitute 1 tablespoon (15 ml) of black truffle oil and ¼ cup (38 g) of goat cheese. A 1-ounce (28-g) black Perigord truffle can cost anywhere from $25 to $40 and can be stored for up to 7 days. Simply bury in a closed container filled with uncooked rice. Later, when you cook the rice, enjoy a beautifully refined taste and aroma.

(continued)

— B'S COOKING TIPS —

Risotto, Refined

Risotto is such a beautiful creamy rice that, when cooked to perfection, can easily cause you to forgo simple white rice. It goes with everything, tastes amazing and is just so velvety. But don't think the hype makes it that cooperative. I consider it an emotional rice that has to be tended to. There are some tricks to always consider when cooking conventionally. Longer cook times and constant supervision chip away at its appealing glory. In the pressure cooker, however, those slightly cumbersome details are completely eliminated. I love that! But there are still a few things to keep in mind when you're making it. Regardless of how you make risotto, the end result should be creamy, not too dry, not too wet and, depending on your palate, should have an al dente firmness. Here are a few helpful tips to keep in mind.

1. If the risotto is too wet, allow it to sit in the cooker for a few minutes, uncovered. 3 to 4 minutes, max, should be enough time. The rice will absorb the water it held on to while cooking. If too dry, add ¼ cup (60 ml) of water or stock and stir well. Maintain on low heat for 5 minutes, also uncovered.

2. If your rice stuck a bit to the bottom of the pot, gently scrape it without getting the superbrowned parts. Ideally, this shouldn't happen, but if you're working with a stovetop cooker, depending on your range or the intensity of its heat, you may have a bit of overcooked rice at the bottom. Practice will also yield perfect risotto.

3. Grate some Parmesan for a bit of a cheesy bite. You can add a little bit of room-temperate butter to your hot risotto for a creamier and even silkier finish.

4. White wine is superb for making risotto. Most any Italian- or French-style recipe lists white wine. It's what I use for all of mine. But if you're like me, and wonder why you have leftover Champagne or sparkling wine the next day, use it! Bubbly is a great substitute for dry white cooking wine. You know it's a shame to waste good bubbly!

SPINACH AND ALMOND RISOTTO

If you don't love spinach, I guarantee this will change your mind. In this recipe, the complementary crunch from the almonds is the perfect counter to a softer vegetable. Add some diced chicken for a more complete and simple meal.

SERVES 4 TO 6

2 tbsp (28 ml) olive oil

1 large onion, diced

6 cloves garlic, minced

3 cups (710 ml) Simple Vegetable Broth (page 157), or store-bought

½ cup (120 ml) dry white wine

2 tbsp (28 g) unsalted butter

2 cups (390 g) uncooked Arborio rice

3 cups (90 g) baby spinach

1 tbsp (15 ml) hot sauce

1 tsp (6 g) salt, or to taste

½ tsp freshly ground white pepper, or to taste

½ cup (72 g) almond halves, divided

Heat the oil in the stovetop pressure cooker over low-medium or use the simmer setting for the electric pressure cooker. Add the onion and garlic and sweat the onion until translucent, about 5 minutes. Add the vegetable broth and bring to a light boil. Add the white wine and butter and stir, using a wooden spoon. Cook for 1 minute, uncovered, over medium heat for the stovetop cooker, or cancel cooking for the electric cooker. Add the rice and remaining ingredients, except ¼ cup (36 g) of the almonds. Stir well and close the lid.

Stovetop: Set to high pressure (15 PSI) and cook over high heat for 10 minutes total.

Electric: Set to high pressure (10–12 PSI) and 12 minutes.

While the risotto is cooking, toast the remaining ¼ cup (36 g) of almonds. When the risotto is done, remove from the heat or turn off the cooker and allow the pressure to release on its own (natural-release). When all of the pressure is out, open the cooker and gently stir the risotto, using a large wooden spoon. Adjust for salt, if necessary. Garnish with the toasted almonds.

*See photo on page 84.

COCONUT CURRY AND CHICKEN RISOTTO

The combination of coconut milk, curry and basil is a beautiful tradition in Thai cuisine. In the Caribbean islands, the former two are also very popular. I've always loved how well they compose a dish. This lovely risotto is a great way to introduce delicate flavors from around the world.

SERVES 4

¼ cup (35 g) salted cashews (sliced or pieces)

1 tbsp (14 g) butter

2 tbsp (28 ml) olive oil

1½ lb (680 g) thin chicken breasts, cut into 1" (2.5-cm) wide strips

1 medium yellow onion, diced

2 tsp (4 g) grated fresh ginger

5 cloves garlic, minced

3 cups (710 ml) Herbed Chicken Stock (page 166), or store-bought

½ cup (120 ml) white cooking wine

1½ tsp (9 g) salt, or to taste

½ cup (120 ml) coconut milk

1 tbsp (6 g) curry powder

3 tbsp (7.5 g) fresh basil, finely chopped, or 1 tbsp (2 g) dried, plus additional for garnish

1½ cups (293 g) uncooked Arborio rice, washed and rinsed

Toast the cashews with the butter in a small nonstick skillet. Remove from the heat and set aside. Heat the olive oil in the stovetop pressure cooker over medium-high or use the sauté setting for the electric pressure cooker. Lightly cook the chicken, onion, ginger and garlic, about 4 minutes. Add the chicken broth and cooking wine, and season with salt. Stir, using a wooden spoon, and bring to a light boil. Add the coconut milk, curry powder and basil. Add the rice and stir to combine all of the ingredients. Cancel cooking for the electric cooker, and close the lid.

Stovetop: Set to high pressure (15 PSI) and cook over high heat for 12 minutes total.

Electric: Set to high pressure (10–12 PSI) and 13 to 14 minutes.

When done, remove from the heat or turn off the cooker and release the pressure, using auto-release.

When all of the pressure is out, open the cooker and gently stir the risotto, using a large wooden spoon. Adjust for salt. Transfer the risotto to a serving bowl and garnish with the toasted cashews and additional basil, if desired.

EVERYDAY WHITE RICE

African, Latin and most Asian cultures swear by rice. Any kind of rice. It's a simple must-have for most meals. It gives me life. It is the perfect answer to a hungry moment with limited time to even think about what I can eat. The pressure cooker helps expedite dinners based on rice. A ten-minute process will provide many options for any day of the week.

SERVES 4 TO 6

2 cups (390 g) uncooked long-grain white rice

2½ cups (590 ml) cold water

½ medium white onion, diced

1 tbsp (15 ml) canola oil

1 tsp (6 g) kosher salt

Wash and rinse the rice, discarding any bad grains. Add all of the ingredients to the cooker. Stir and close the lid.

Stovetop: Set to low pressure (8 PSI) and cook over high heat for 8 to 9 minutes total.

Electric: Use the rice setting, or set to low pressure (5–8 PSI) and 6 minutes.

When done, remove from the heat or turn off the cooker and allow the pressure to release on its own (natural-release), about 4 minutes. When all of the pressure is out, open the cooker and fluff the rice, using a fork. Adjust for salt.

RICE AND OKRA

Rice and okra are two individual ingredients I ate a lot as a child. My mother was very adamant my siblings and I got our appropriate share of daily vegetables. You can enjoy okra's funky shape and great taste in many different foods. I love how it pairs with this seasoned Spanish rice. No slime, lots of texture and seven minutes' cook time make it a golden option.

SERVES 6

⅓ cup (80 ml) canola oil

1 cup (160 g) diced Spanish onion

2 large cloves garlic, mashed

½ green bell pepper, diced

½ cup (60 g) fresh curly parsley leaves, plus more for garnish, if desired

16 oz (455 g) frozen okra, rinsed and patted dry

2 tsp (5 g) achiote or annatto powder or oil

1½ cups (355 ml) Herbed Chicken Stock (page 166), or store-bought

1½ cups (293 g) uncooked long-grain white rice

1 tsp (6 g) kosher salt

Heat the oil over medium for the stovetop pressure cooker or use the simmer setting for the electric pressure cooker. Add the onion, garlic, bell pepper and parsley. Reduce the heat to low for the stovetop cooker, or maintain the simmer setting for the electric cooker; sweat the onions for about 3 minutes. Add, stir and cook the okra with the achiote or annatto seasoning over medium heat for the stovetop cooker or cancel cooking for the electric cooker, cooking with the residual heat, about 2 minutes. Add the chicken stock and rice, season with the salt and stir. Close the lid.

Stovetop: Set to low pressure (8 PSI) and cook over high heat for 7 minutes total.

Electric: Set to low _high_ pressure (5–8 PSI) and 13 minutes.

When done, remove from the heat or turn off the cooker and release the pressure, using auto-release. Garnish with parsley, if desired.

VIBRANT YELLOW VEGETABLE RICE

This simple rice recipe could easily be in the "Classic and Fusion Plates from My Cuban Kitchen" chapter, considering how much I still eat it. Second to white rice, it's the most common rice you'll find in many Latin homes. Its vibrancy and subtle smokiness makes it a great option for enjoying with roasted chicken or blackened salmon. Splash a bit of garlic hot sauce on it and you'll heighten the flavor. I never eat this rice without hot sauce. Try it!

SERVES 4 TO 6

¼ cup (60 ml) canola oil

1 Spanish onion, diced

½ green bell pepper, diced

4 cloves garlic, minced

1 tsp (5 g) bijol *seasoning*

½ cup (123 g) tomato sauce

1 cup (455 g) frozen vegetables

1½ cups (355 ml) water or Simple Vegetable Broth (page 157)

1½ cups (293 g) uncooked white rice

1 tbsp (18 g) kosher salt

Fresh cilantro, for garnish (optional)

Heat the oil in the stovetop pressure cooker over medium-high or use the sauté setting for the electric pressure cooker. Sauté the onion, bell pepper, garlic and *bijol* until very fragrant, about 3 minutes. Stir in the tomato sauce and reduce the heat to low-medium for the stovetop pressure cooker or cancel the sauté setting and reset to the steam setting for the electric pressure cooker, and cook for 2 minutes. Add the vegetables, water or vegetable broth, rice and salt. Cancel cooking for the electric cooker, stir and close the lid.

Stovetop: Set to low pressure (8 PSI) and cook over medium heat for 10 minutes total.

Electric: Use the rice setting, or set to low pressure (5–8 PSI) and 11–12 minutes.

When done, remove from the heat or turn off the cooker and allow the pressure to release on its own (natural-release). When all of the pressure is out, open the cooker and fluff the rice with a wooden fork. Allow the rice to sit for 5 minutes, uncovered. Garnish with cilantro, if desired.

B'S COOKING TIP: *Bijol* is a traditional coloring spice blend used in a lot of Latin cuisine. It offers a detectable but subtle flavor and is great for adding red and yellow tones to foods. In lieu of *bijol*, use 1 (5-gram [1-teaspoon]) packet of Sazón with achiote, another coloring spice (see page 212), or 1 teaspoon (5 ml) achiote oil (see page 29).

GARLICKY AND CUMIN BROWN RICE

Invite more brown rice in your diet with this easy recipe. You can really enjoy it more often in the pressure cooker. It's superearthy and ultrafragrant on its own. Use this for recipes you've traditionally made with white rice. I love pairing it with the Savory Eggplant and Potato Mélange (page 146).

SERVES 4

1 tbsp (15 ml) olive oil

6 cloves garlic, thinly sliced

2 tsp (4 g) cumin seeds

1½ cups (293 g) uncooked brown rice

2 cups (475 ml) Simple Vegetable Broth (page 157), or store-bought

1 tsp (5 ml) canola oil

½ tsp salt

½ cup (30 g) chopped fresh cilantro or parsley, for garnish

Heat the oil in the stovetop pressure cooker over medium-high or use the sauté setting for the electric pressure cooker. Sauté the garlic and cumin seeds until fragrant, about 2 minutes. Add and stir the rice, vegetable broth, oil and salt to taste. Cancel cooking for the electric cooker, and close the lid.

Stovetop: Set to high pressure (15 PSI) and cook over high heat for 15 minutes total. Once the pressure point has been reached, lower the heat to medium or enough to maintain pressure.

Electric: Set to high pressure (10–12 PSI) and 20 minutes. If you have a brown rice setting, you may use that.

When done, remove from the heat or turn off the cooker and allow the pressure to release on its own (natural-release), about 8 to 9 minutes. Open the cooker and fluff the rice, using a fork. Adjust for salt. Garnish with parsley or cilantro for added color and fragrance.

Herbed Ghost Rice with Sun-Dried Tomato

I can guarantee you this is one of the easiest recipes you will make and enjoy in this book. A private client gave me a bag of "ghost" wild rice to test out. I had never seen it but instantly loved the uncooked texture. It had a great aesthetic and aroma. I ended up making it for my mother who loves wild rice more than our classic long-grain white. I tweaked a basic recipe and came up with this earthy and slightly acidic version, which turned out nuttier and rounder than I anticipated. It pairs really well with a lighter protein. A seared Ahi tuna would be wonderful.

Serves 4 to 6

2 cups (390 g) uncooked ghost wild rice

2½ cups (590 ml) water or Simple Vegetable Broth (page 157)

2 tbsp (28 g) tomato paste

1 cup (160 g) finely diced yellow onion

¼ cup (14 g) sun-dried tomatoes, chopped

1 tsp (2 g) herbes de Provence

⅛ tsp ground cumin

1 tbsp (15 ml) canola oil

1 tsp (6 g) salt, or to taste

Wash and rinse the rice. Add all of the ingredients to the cooker in the order listed and stir to combine well. Close the lid.

Stovetop: Set to high pressure (15 PSI) and cook over high heat for 12 minutes total. Once the pressure point has been reached, lower the heat to medium or enough to maintain pressure.

Electric: Use the wild or brown rice setting, or set to high pressure (10–12 PSI) and 15 minutes.

When done, remove from the heat or turn off the cooker and allow the pressure to release on its own (natural-release), about 8 to 9 minutes. When all of the pressure is out, open the cooker and fluff the rice, separating the grains using a fork.

STEEL-CUT OATMEAL, 3 WAYS

I love the idea of customizing my oatmeal with endless options. All you need is to know the basic process of softening steel-cut oats into a creamy bowl to which you can add to your heart's content. The following two recipes are throwback flavors we've all enjoyed at some point. The third is my new favorite; you'll appreciate the freshness of fruit and added texture with the nuts. Once you get the hang of the pressure points for your amount, play around with your ingredients.

Peaches and Cream

These were the first ever steel-cut oats I made as a way to convince my sister that instant peaches and cream was gimmicky and not really the best there was. Truthfully, I loved those little packs, too, while growing up. They were so easy to take anywhere I went. But when I figured out I could tweak my own, inclusive of ending up with the perfect oatmeal, I knew my breakfast experience would change forever.

SERVES 6

3 tbsp (42 g) butter

3 tbsp (45 g) light brown sugar

2 peaches, peeled, pitted and cubed in ½"
(1.3-cm) pieces

1 tsp (5 ml) pure vanilla extract

2 cups (475 ml) water

1 cup (235 ml) heavy whipping cream

1½ cups (120 g) steel-cut oats

⅛ tsp kosher salt

Freshly grated nutmeg (optional)

Pure maple syrup (optional)

Heat the butter and sugar in the stovetop pressure cooker over low-medium or use the simmer setting for the electric pressure cooker. Add the peaches and vanilla extract and coat the fruit well, using a rubber or silicone spatula. Stir in the water, cream, oats and salt. Cancel cooking for the electric cooker, stir and close the lid.

Stovetop: Set to high pressure (15 PSI) and set the timer for 20 minutes. Cook over high heat until the pressure point has been reached, then lower the heat to low-medium and continue to cook.

Electric: Set to high pressure (10–12 PSI) and 15 minutes.

When done, remove the stovetop cooker from the heat and apply quick-release, or turn off the electric cooker and apply auto-release. When all of the pressure is out, open the cooker and stir to combine well, gently scraping any oatmeal off the sides.

Sprinkle individual servings with nutmeg and drizzle with maple syrup, if desired.

Warm Apple and Pecan

The Delicious Apple and Kiwi Sauce recipe (page 205) inspired this oatmeal. I was enjoying the ease of that seven-minute deliciousness and thought it perfect to do something with them for colder weather. This combo works for pies, so why not for a breakfast with less calories or carbs?! Play with your apple choice and enjoy a fruity and nutty bowl of oats every time oatmeal's in order. For an added touch of herbal essence, chop fresh sage and cook into the butter and apples.

SERVES 6

3 tbsp (42 g) butter

1 tsp (2.5 g) ground cinnamon

2 medium Granny Smith apples, seeded and cut into medium dice

3 to 4 fresh sage leaves, chiffonaded (optional)

2 tbsp (30 g) light brown sugar

1 cup (110 g) pecans, chopped

1½ cups (120 g) steel-cut oats

3 cups (710 ml) water

½ cup (120 ml) heavy whipping cream

½ cup (120 ml) apple cider

Salt

Pure maple syrup (optional)

Add the butter, cinnamon and apples to the cooker. Heat in the stovetop pressure cooker over high, or use the sauté setting for the electric pressure cooker, stirring constantly, about 2 minutes. For the stovetop cooker, lower the heat to medium, or cancel the sauté setting for the electric cooker. Stir in the brown sugar and coat the apples well. Stir in the pecans. Add the oats and cover with the water, cream, cider and a pinch of salt. Stir well. Close the lid.

Stovetop: Set to high pressure (15 PSI) and set the timer for 20 minutes. Cook over high heat until the pressure has been reached, then lower the heat to low-medium and continue to cook.

Electric: Set to high pressure (10–12 PSI) and 15 minutes.

When done, remove the stovetop cooker from the heat and apply quick-release, or turn off the electric cooker and apply auto-release. When all of the pressure is out, open the cooker and stir to combine well, gently scraping any oatmeal off the sides.

Dust individual servings with additional cinnamon and drizzle with maple syrup, if desired.

B'S COOKING TIP: For denser oatmeal, cook over low heat after all of the pressure is released, about 5 minutes. For a thinner oatmeal, stir in an additional ½ to 1 cup (120 to 235 ml) equal parts apple cider and heavy whipping cream, after all the pressure is released.

(continued)

Lavender and Berries

Of these three oatmeal recipes, this is my favorite one. I'm currently obsessing over all things lavender, wondering how many dishes I can add it to or how many infusions I can make. Blueberries are always a great idea and raspberries are my favorite berry of all time. Make this as fragrant as you'd like by adding two more teaspoons (1 g) of lavender.

SERVES 4

3 cups (710 ml) water

½ cup (120 ml) heavy whipping cream

2 tbsp (30 g) light brown sugar

1 tbsp (1.5 g) culinary-grade lavender flowers, divided, plus more to garnish, if desired

1 cup (80 g) steel-cut oats

½ cup (77 g) frozen blueberries

Pinch of salt

1 cup (145 g) fresh blueberries

1 cup (125 g) fresh raspberries

2 tbsp (28 ml) pure maple syrup, plus more to garnish, if desired

1 tsp (2 g) ground cinnamon

Add the water, cream, brown sugar and 2 teaspoons (1 g) of the lavender to the cooker. Stir and bring to a boil over high heat for the stovetop pressure cooker, or use the sauté setting for the electric pressure cooker, about 3 minutes. Stir in the oats, frozen blueberries and salt; cancel cooking for the electric cooker, and close the lid.

Stovetop: Set to high pressure (15 PSI) and set the timer for 18 minutes. Cook over high heat until the pressure has been reached, then lower the heat to low-medium and continue to cook.

Electric: Set to high pressure (10–12 PSI) and 12 minutes.

While the oats are cooking, make the fruit mixture: In a small mixing bowl, combine the fresh berries, remaining 1 teaspoon (0.5 g) of lavender and the maple syrup. Stir and set aside.

When the oats are done, remove the stovetop cooker from the heat and apply quick-release, or turn off the electric cooker and apply auto-release. When all of the pressure is out, open the cooker and stir in additional maple syrup, if desired, using a wooden spoon.

Serve in individual bowls. Sprinkle each with cinnamon and 2 tablespoons (20 g) of the fresh berry mixture. Garnish with additional lavender flowers, if desired. For creamier oatmeal, stir in 1 to 2 tablespoons (15 to 28 ml) of heavy whipping cream while warm.

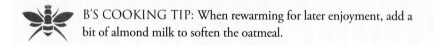 B'S COOKING TIP: When rewarming for later enjoyment, add a bit of almond milk to soften the oatmeal.

Mushroom Quinoa

I didn't get into quinoa when the trend hit. It took me about another year before I was convinced. Quinoa is an ancient grain hailing from Peru. It's wonderful and extremely easy to use with and in different foods. This recipe is hearty, bold and has lovely texture offered by the mix of gourmet mushrooms. I love the idea of a runny egg on top, though the picture doesn't show it. Even without the mushrooms, this quinoa is basic enough to build on; add some of your favorite ingredients. Some ideas are tofu, chicken or falafel.

SERVES 4 TO 6

1 cup (173 g) uncooked white or red quinoa

2 tbsp (28 ml) olive oil

½ cup (80 g) red onion, diced

2–3 garlic cloves, finely minced

3 cups (210 g) stemmed and sliced wild mushrooms or gourmet blend

1 cup (235 ml) Simple Vegetable Broth (page 157), or store-bought

¼ tsp dried sage

½ tsp kosher salt

¼ tsp garlic salt

Fresh curly parsley, for garnish

Wash and rinse the quinoa, straining through a cheesecloth. Transfer the quinoa to the pressure cooker. Heat the quinoa in the stovetop pressure cooker over high or use the sauté setting of the electric pressure cooker, stirring constantly with a wire whisk, until the water from rinsing has evaporated, about 4 minutes. The quinoa will start to pop when it is dry. Cancel the electric cooker once the quinoa has started to pop. Add the olive oil, onion, garlic, then the mushrooms and sauté for 1 minute over medium-high heat for the stovetop pressure cooker or with the electric pressure cooker off but still warm. Stir in the vegetable broth and season with the dried sage and the kosher and garlic salts. Close the lid.

Stovetop: Set to high pressure (15 PSI) and set the timer for 6 minutes total. Cook over high heat until the pressure point is reached, then reduce the heat to medium and finish cooking.

Electric: Set to high pressure (10–12 PSI) and 7–8 minutes.

When done, remove from the heat or turn off the cooker and allow the pressure to release on its own (natural-release), about 5 to 6 minutes, then apply auto-release. When all of the pressure is out, open the cooker, stir and adjust for salt. Garnish each serving with chopped parsley.

 B CREATIVE! Eat this warm as is, or chill for later and use in a salad of your choice. Mix in kale, broccoli, cherry tomatoes, cucumber and slices of Haas avocado. You can also add to your chicken soup in lieu of rice!

HERBED COCONUT COD RICE

One my favorite "I'm too busy to cook" dinners is fluffy white rice, sliced tomatoes and a can of tuna flaked into the rice. Drizzle a bit of olive oil and black pepper and I am one happy person. This is my upgraded version with a hint of Caribbean flair. It's perfumed and delicate but filling. I'd still slice tomatoes on the side!

SERVES 4

2 tbsp (28 ml) olive oil

½ red bell pepper, diced

¼ cup (25 g) diced spring onion

½ cup (80 g) diced white onion

2 cloves garlic, minced

1 cup (235 ml) coconut milk

⅛ tsp crushed red pepper flakes

1½ lbs (680 g) unsalted cod, cut into 1–1½" (2.5–3.8-cm) pieces

2 tsp (1 g) dried parsley

2 tsp (12 g) sea salt

1½ cups (293 g) uncooked long-grain white rice

1 cup (235 ml) water

3 tbsp (15 g) sweetened coconut flakes, plus 1 tbsp (5 g) toasted for garnish (optional)

½ bunch fresh parsley, for garnish

Heat the oil in the stovetop pressure cooker over high or use the sauté setting for the electric pressure cooker. Sauté the bell pepper, spring onion, white onion and garlic until fragrant, about 3 minutes. Stir in the coconut milk and red pepper flakes and lower the heat to low-medium for the stovetop pressure cooker or cancel cooking for the electric pressure cooker. Gently add the cod. Add the parsley and season with salt. Add the rice and water and sprinkle in the coconut flakes. Gently spread out the fish, using a wooden spoon. Close the lid.

Stovetop: Set to low pressure (8 PSI) and cook over medium heat for 11 minutes total.

Electric: Use the rice setting, or set to low pressure (5–8 PSI) and 12 minutes.

When done, remove from the heat or turn off the cooker and allow the pressure to release on its own (natural-release). When all of the pressure is out, open the cooker and gently fluff the rice with a fork. Adjust for salt. Garnish with fresh parsley and toasted coconut flakes if desired.

Decadent 4-Cheese Truffle Mac and Cheese

You might rightfully conclude I really love truffles since several recipes in this cookbook use them, but it's not very often I indulge and buy a pricey gem. That's where good-quality truffle oil reigns. A drizzle here and there in this ultracreamy mac and cheese is subtle enough to complement the robust cheese combo, but present enough to make an impact.

SERVES 6

4 tbsp (55 g) butter, divided

1 cup (160 g) finely minced onion

1 shallot, minced

1 tbsp (3 g) dried thyme

2 tsp (1 g) dried basil, or 2½ tbsp (6 g) fresh

1 quart (496 ml) Simple Vegetable Broth (page 157), or store-bought

2¼ cups (532 ml) half-and-half, divided

1 lb (455 g) or 5 cups pasta of choice (medium elbow or penne)

Salt and freshly ground black pepper

1 cup (115 g) shredded cheddar cheese (medium grate), divided

1 cup (115 g) shredded extra-sharp cheddar cheese (medium grate)

1 cup (120 g) shredded smoked Gouda cheese (medium grate)

1 cup (120 g) shredded Havarti cheese (medium grate)

2 tbsp (15 ml) white truffle oil

1 cup (115 g) unseasoned panko bread crumbs

Preheat the oven to 350°F (180°C). Heat 2 tablespoons (28 g) of the butter in the stovetop pressure cooker over medium-high or use the sauté setting for the electric pressure cooker. Lightly sauté the onion, shallot, thyme and basil, about 2 minutes. Whisk in the vegetable broth and 2 cups (455 ml) of the half-and-half. Add the pasta and season to taste with salt and pepper. Cancel cooking for the electric cooker, and close the lid.

Stovetop: Set to high pressure (15 PSI) and cook over high heat for 7 minutes total.

Electric: Set to high pressure (10–12 PSI) and 7 minutes.

When done, remove from the heat or turn off the cooker and allow the pressure to release on its own (natural-release), about 5 to 6 minutes. When all of the pressure is out, open the cooker and stir in all the cheeses, except ½ cup (58 g) of the cheddar cheese, until everything is well combined. With remaining 2 tablespoons (28 g) of butter, grease a 9 x 13-inch (23 x 33-cm) pan or casserole. Transfer the pasta to the prepared pan and spread out evenly. Pour the remaining ¼ cup (60 ml) of half-and-half over the top. Cover with the remaining ½ cup (58 g) of cheddar cheese. Drizzle with the truffle oil and top evenly with the panko crumbs. Bake, uncovered, for 10 minutes, or until the panko is golden and toasty.

B IN THE KNOW! Most truffle oils are only infusions of the aroma and not made with real truffles. Some are poorly manufactured and will be extremely pungent, almost undesirable. A good truffle oil will have visible bits and shavings of real black truffle. You should be able to find some at local gourmet stores or online. Depending on where you live, most home goods stores with gourmet food sections will carry it. I've been successful in finding it there.

Mushroom and Turkey Ragout

Have you ever tried reverse engineering a recipe? Or Googled it to come up short? This recipe is that for me. I had a $6 bowl of rich and creamy turkey ragout about eight years ago that left an impression strong enough to test and retest. It finally worked. It's a bit laborious, but worth it. I hope you're inspired to make your own pasta sauces, such as the one in this recipe. They're incredibly rewarding. I love this one for its meatiness, earthiness and all around richness. The turkey is wonderful and lean, but you can always opt for beef.

Serves 6

1 tbsp (15 ml) canola oil

1 cup (160 g) diced onion

4 cloves garlic, minced

⅛ tsp dried cumin

1 cup (235 ml) Simple Vegetable Broth (page 157), or store-bought

½ cup (123 g) tomato sauce

2 carrots, chopped

2 stalks celery, chopped

2 tbsp (5 g) fresh basil, finely chopped, plus more, thinly sliced for garnish, or 2 tsp (1 g) dried

1 lb (455 g) 80/20 ground turkey

1½ tsp (9 g) kosher salt

¼ tsp freshly ground black pepper

7 cremini mushrooms, stemmed and sliced

¼ tsp crushed red pepper flakes

½ cup (120 ml) heavy whipping cream

¼ cup (60 ml) olive oil

Shaved Pecorino Romano or Parmesan cheese, for garnish

Heat the canola oil in the stovetop pressure cooker over high or use the sauté setting for the electric pressure cooker. Sauté the onion and garlic, seasoning with the cumin, until fragrant, about 3 minutes. Stir in the vegetable broth and tomato sauce and cook for 1 minute. Add the carrots, celery and basil. Stir, cancel cooking for the electric cooker and close the lid.

Stovetop: Set to high pressure (15 PSI) and cook over high heat for 7 minutes total.

Electric: Set to high pressure (10–12 PSI) and 7 minutes.

When done, remove from the heat or cancel cooking and release the pressure, using auto-release.

While the vegetables are cooking, brown the turkey in a skillet over medium heat, seasoning it with the salt and black pepper, about 4 minutes. Separate the meat, using a wooden fork, making sure to break down the clumps. Add the mushrooms and cook over medium heat, about 5 minutes. Remove from the heat and set aside.

Transfer the vegetable sauce to a high-powered food processor and purée until the mixture is completely smooth, about 2 minutes. Transfer the turkey mixture and the vegetable sauce back to the pressure cooker and stir to combine. Add the crushed red pepper flakes and adjust for salt. Slowly whisk in the cream and olive oil. Close the lid.

Stovetop: Set to high pressure (15 PSI) and cook over high heat for 5 minutes total.

Electric: Set to high pressure (10–12 PSI) and 5 minutes.

When finished, turn off the heat or turn off the cooker and release the pressure, using slow auto-release (refer to page 19 if needed). Serve the ragout over wheat angel hair, linguine or your choice of pasta. Garnish with thinly sliced basil and the Pecorino Romano or Parmesan cheese.

CLASSIC AND FUSION PLATES FROM MY CUBAN KITCHEN

I love Cuban food. Our cuisine is my favorite. I am a bit biased, honestly. Although our food lacks deeply authentic and indigenous roots, the combination of African, Spanish and French make it a lovely blend of techniques, textures and flavors. That unique combination makes an internationally desired palate. Almost all of the dishes in this chapter are true to their original recipe as passed down from my late grandmother Violeta—whose garden in East Havana was impressive, replete with herbs and vegetables that made her modest concrete house look more like a CSA greenhouse than a private home—and my mother, my personal culinary goddess. Maintaining the integrity of these recipes is my way of honoring the two women who have encouraged my kitchen musings. My mother's grace and finesse in the kitchen were so attractive it drew me to want to emulate her. Everything she dished out touched my soul. I still react to her food in a way few others can elicit.

You'll note a lot of the meat dishes in this chapter have similar ingredients. That's not by accident. With the limited food resources in postrevolutionary Cuba, people had to be efficient with their sundries. While the basic ingredients are very similar, each dish finishes differently as the proteins have different muscle structure and fat, two characteristics that contribute to their delicious uniqueness. The consistency in ingredients throughout results in classic dishes that are distinguishably Cuban no matter where you enjoy them, thus rendering them absolute staples, passed down from generation to generation. My favorite dish to make is my mother's version of the famed *rabo encendido* or Braised Peppered Red Wine Oxtail (page 112). I've put my personal spin on it, which she applauds. Once you have mastered it, it should be succulent enough to fall off the stubby bone. I also encourage you to play around with your vegetable choices in the *pollo en fricasé* or Chicken Fricassee (page 128), a pot that beautifully represents the essence of Cuban cuisine. It's also the one dish that kicked off my professional cooking career. These dishes are a poetic piece of my soul. I hope you love them.

FRAGRANT SAFFRON BRAISED CHICKEN AND RICE

Arroz con Pollo

Arroz con pollo is one of our more common dinners. All home cooks have a version they swear by, depending on the region of Cuba where they come from and their access to certain ingredients. Pressure cookers are especially useful when making large amounts of food for the family since it's done in about 25 minutes faster than in a typical iron *casuela*. The beauty of this dish is the garnish—traditionally, bright red strips of pimiento or smoked *piquillo* peppers, and scattered *petits pois*.

SERVES 4 TO 6

1 tsp (1 g) saffron threads plus 3 tbsp (45 ml) warm water

2 lb (905 g) skinless and boneless chicken thighs, cut into quarters

2 tsp (12 g) kosher salt

5 cloves garlic, pressed

¼ cup (60 ml) vegetable oil

½ red bell pepper, diced

1 medium Spanish onion, diced

½ tsp ground cumin

1 tsp (1 g) dried oregano

2 cups (475 ml) Herbed Chicken Stock (page 166), or store-bought

1½ cups (293 g) uncooked long-grain white rice

½ cup (72 g) sliced pimiento or smoked piquillo *peppers, for garnish*

½ cup (112 g) sweet peas, drained, for garnish

In a small bowl, add the saffron threads to the warm water and set aside. Clean and pat dry the chicken. Rub the chicken all over with the salt and garlic. If you have time, cover and chill for 30 minutes. Heat the stovetop pressure cooker over medium-high or use the browning setting for the electric pressure cooker, and add the oil. Add the chicken and brown on all sides, about 3 minutes. Reduce the heat to medium for the stovetop cooker or cancel the browning setting and reset to the steam setting for the electric cooker. Add the bell pepper and onion. Stir, using a wooden spoon, and cook for 3 minutes. Add the cumin, oregano and chicken stock. Bring to a light to medium boil and cook for 5 minutes. Add the rice and the saffron mixture. Stir gently, cancel cooking for the electric cooker and close the lid.

Stovetop: Set to high pressure (15 PSI) and cook over medium heat for 15 minutes total.

Electric: Set to high pressure (10–12 PSI) and 17 to 18 minutes.

When done, remove from the heat or off turn the cooker and allow the pressure to release on its own (natural-release). When all of the pressure is out, open the cooker and fluff the rice, using a fork. Serve the rice on a large platter. Garnish with the sliced pimiento or *piquillo* peppers and sweet peas.

B'S COOKING TIP: Traditionally, I finish off this beautiful rice dish with a good-quality beer, which adds another level of flavor. Evenly pour 1 cup (235 ml) of beer all over the rice when it's done. Keep the cooker open. Turn the heat to low for the stovetop cooker or use the warm or steam setting for the electric cooker, and allow the rice to rest for 5 minutes. Continue with the recipe.

BRAISED PEPPERED RED WINE OXTAIL

Rabo Encendido

Much like my mother's famous black beans, I've waited a long time to publicly share this recipe. In 2008, I teased America when I served my family dinner on Chef Emeril Lagasse's show *Emeril Green* on the Discovery Channel. That particular scene was long enough to put it on the map. Yes, it's very popular and well known as a beloved Cuban dish, but this one is extraordinary. I've played with different versions over the years and settled on one that appeals to both refined and more novel palates. Oxtail is a beautiful delicacy whose succulent and tender characteristics render it a favorite. It's so decadent, you'll want the pressure cooker to dish this out in about 45 minutes and not two hours. Serve with fluffy white rice or creamy mashed potato or simply enjoy the robustness with grilled vegetables.

SERVES 4 TO 5

3 lb (1.4 kg) oxtail

1 tbsp (18 g) kosher salt

¼ cup (60 ml) canola oil

1½ cups (368 g) tomato sauce, or
3 medium tomatoes, puréed

1 cup (235 ml) red wine (Cabernet or
Shiraz)

1 green bell pepper, cut into ½" (1.3-cm)
julienne

1 Spanish onion, cut into ½" (1.3-cm)
julienne

5 cloves garlic, minced

3 tbsp (45 ml) white vinegar

2 tsp (4 g) freshly ground black pepper

½ tsp ground cumin

1 tsp (1 g) dried oregano

2 sprigs rosemary

1 bay leaf

Clean the oxtail, minimally trimming any excess fat, using a paring knife. Some fat is good as it will render and add flavor to the sauce. Season the oxtail with the salt. Heat the oil in the stovetop pressure cooker over high or use the browning setting for the electric pressure cooker. Add the oxtail to the cooker and brown on all sides, about 3 minutes. Add all of the remaining ingredients to the cooker and gently stir. Cancel cooking for the electric cooker, and close the lid.

Stovetop: Set to high pressure (15 PSI) and set the timer to 35 minutes. Cook over high heat until the pressure point is reached, then lower the heat to medium and continue to cook.

Electric: Set to the stew setting and adjust the time to add an additional 5 minutes, or set to high pressure (10–12 PSI) and 40 minutes.

When done, remove from the heat or turn off the cooker and allow the pressure to release on its own (natural-release), about 12 minutes. If the pressure is not fully out at 12 minutes, turn the valve to auto-release. When all of the pressure is out, open the cooker and gently stir. Adjust for salt and pepper.

*See photo on page 108.

 B CREATIVE! Another fantastic way to enjoy oxtails is to braise them and pull the meat from the bone to make oxtail patties. Bread and pan-fry them. Serve with the Black Truffle Cheese Risotto on page 86.

CLASSIC TUBER AND BEEF RIB STEW

Ajiaco

Ajiaco is a really typical root tuber and meat stew enjoyed in all of Cuba and usually reserved for special occasions, historically for certain festivals. It dates back to as early as the 1500s and is still incredibly common, though I didn't eat it much while growing up. We ate tubers individually, mostly as rich mashes. Unlike our other stews or *potajes*, *ajiaco* doesn't have the ultrathick consistency and density you'll see in the beans dishes. But the starchy tubers make it thicker and denser than a vegetable soup. The pressure cooker truly comes in handy when wanting dishes that can normally take all day. I don't eat pork and have enough oxtail in other meals, so I opted for beef ribs, which are nice and fatty. You can add oxtails and pork ribs for an even more robust stew. Chicken is always acceptable and adds contrast with the beef. I personally love how the plantain stands out among so many vegetables. Enjoy it on its own, but ladling it over rice is always a good idea.

SERVES 6

1½ lb (680 g) beef ribs

1 fresh or frozen yuca root, peeled, cut into 2" (5-cm) equal-size pieces

1 cup (140 g) seeded and cubed butternut squash or pumpkin (1½" [4-cm] cubes)

1 midripe plantain, cut in 1½" (4-cm) pieces

1 large malanga (similar to white taro root), peeled and cut into 2" (5-cm) equal-size pieces

1 ñame (similar to white yam), peeled and cut into 2" (5-cm) equal-size pieces

1 Spanish onion, quartered

2 cloves garlic, left whole

½ green bell pepper, chopped

2 white potatoes, peeled, cut into 1½" (4-cm) chunks

1 ear corn, cut into thirds

1 large tomato, quartered

5 sprigs cilantro

1 tbsp (18 g) kosher salt

2¼ quarts (2.1 L) water or Herbed Beef Stock (page 167)

1 boniato (white sweet potato), peeled and cut into 1½" (5-cm) equal-size pieces (optional; see tip)

Add all of the ingredients to the cooker in the order listed. Stir once. Close the lid.

Stovetop: Set to high pressure (15 PSI) and set your timer for 30 minutes. Cook over high heat until the pressure is reached, then lower the heat to medium and continue to cook.

Electric: Set to high pressure (10–12 PSI) and 35 minutes.

When done, remove from the heat or turn off the cooker and allow the pressure to release on its own (natural-release). When all of the pressure is out, open the cooker and adjust for salt. The stew should be thicker than vegetable soup since the tubers are so starchy. If it's too thin, bring to a boil, uncovered, for 5 minutes for the stovetop pressure cooker, or use the simmer setting for the electric pressure cooker. Serve hot and with crusty bread. A few slices of avocado are a nice addition, too.

B'S COOKING TIP: While most traditional *ajiacos* have a few more tubers, I omitted two in my recipe for no other reason than to simplify your shopping! Some of the tubers are really similar and have different names in different countries, such as boniato, malanga, taro, *ñame* and so on, which can be confusing if you don't know them well. If you're stuck and can't find *ñame*, a white yam, opt for the American sweet potato.

THE BEST YUCA IN GARLIC MOJO EVER

Yuca con Mojo

This is the only dish in the world where unlimited amounts of starch and carbs will not faze my conscience. I can eat boiled yuca into destructive oblivion. I love it almost as much as I love my fanciest shoes. I just love it. The pressure cooker breaks down this hard root tuber in no time. It is delicately topped with a robust but bright citrus *mojo* of garlicky goodness. This essential side dish underscores that "less is more." Opt for frozen yuca over fresh. It saves you the trouble of peeling the hard, barklike skin and cooks in just fifteen minutes in the cooker. Conventionally, it can take up to 45 minutes with much more water.

SERVES 6

3 lb (1.4 kg) frozen yuca
3 cups (710 ml) water
1 tbsp (18 g) salt
¼ cup (60 ml) canola oil
1 Spanish onion, sliced
1 bulb garlic, separated into cloves, mashed with skin on
Juice of 1 lemon
Juice of 1 orange

Add the yuca, water and salt to the cooker. Close the lid.

Stovetop: Set to high pressure (15 PSI) and cook over high heat for 15 minutes total.

Electric: Set to high pressure (10–12 PSI) and 15 minutes.

When done, remove from the heat or turn off the cooker and allow the pressure to release on its own (natural-release). While the pressure is releasing, make the *mojo*. In a medium stainless-steel skillet, heat the oil. Sauté the onion and the unpeeled garlic over medium heat until the onion is almost translucent and al dente and the garlic starts to brown, about 3 minutes. It will be very fragrant. Make sure not to char the garlic skin. You're going to use it. Remove from the heat and set aside.

When all of the pressure is out, open the cooker and adjust for salt, stirring gently. Drain, using a colander. It's okay to retain about ¼ cup (60 ml) of yuca water to yield a thinner *mojo*. Because of the starch, it will be somewhat thick and opaque, depending on doneness.

Transfer the yuca to a large, deep serving dish. Smother the yuca with all of the onion and garlic mixture (*mojo*) including the oil and garlic skin, evenly covering it all. Squeeze the lemon and orange juice all over. Discard the citrus. Serve immediately.

B'S COOKING TIP: Cassava root is very starchy, therefore, the water will eventually start to thicken and become opaque. Prevent your yuca from getting too mushy. A good consistency is a mix of al dente and firmly soft—somewhat breakable—but not mashable. If your yuca is too hard, cook for an additional 2 to 3 minutes over high heat on high pressure.

Earthy Split Green Peas

Chícharos

Of all the *potajes* or soups I grew up eating in our very Cuban home, this is by far my favorite. I will hurt someone for a pot of these insanely perfect peas. It's the one dish I seldom make for myself and prefer to have my mother make. When she does, a phone call letting me know they're done immediately alters my day so I can make my way to her house to eat. It has that effect on me. The not-so-pretty green-colored peas are earthy and thick, but velvety and creamy when poured over rice. On their own, this rich stew or soup—I prefer just *potaje*—is rounded with butternut squash (much like the other lighter-colored legumes) and a variety of beef cuts. Flank steak is my default, but try bone-out short ribs or smoked chorizo.

SERVES 6 TO 8

1 Spanish onion, diced

1 red bell pepper, chopped

3 cloves garlic, mashed

3 tbsp (45 ml) olive oil

½ tsp dried oregano

¼ tsp ground cumin

1 bay leaf

2 medium white potatoes, cut into 1" (2.5-cm) cubes

1 cup (140 g) seeded and cubed butternut squash (1" [2.5-cm] cubes)

½ lb (225 g) flank or skirt steak, cut into 2" (5-cm) chunks

7 cups (1.7 L) water or Simple Vegetable Broth (page 157)

16 oz (455 g) dried split green peas

1 tbsp (18 g) kosher salt or to taste

Add the onion, red bell pepper and garlic to a food processor. Pulse for 10 to 20 seconds on medium speed until the vegetables are broken down and you have a semithick mixture. You don't want it to be completely liquefied or too chunky. Heat the olive oil in the stovetop pressure cooker over medium-high or use the sauté function for the electric pressure cooker and sauté the vegetable mixture, seasoning with oregano and cumin, for 2 minutes. Add all of the remaining ingredients, in the order listed, seasoning to taste with salt. Stir well, cancel cooking for the electric cooker and close the lid.

Stovetop: Set to high pressure (15 PSI) and cook over high heat for 15 minutes total.

Electric: Set to high pressure (10–12 PSI) and 15 minutes.

When done, turn off the heat or turn off the electric cooker and allow the pressure to release on its own (natural-release), about 10 minutes.

 B'S COOKING TIP: This will thicken up over the course of a few hours, once it's gotten to room temperature. To enjoy the next day, simply add some broth and warm over low heat.

Red Beans and Rice

Arroz Congrí o Frijoles Colorado

This is arguably the real *arroz congrí*, though any Cuban person you talk to will always refer to black beans and rice as *arroz congrí*. I'm not familiar with the genesis of the discrepancy, but it makes for a good debate among family and friends. The origin of this popular rice is in Haiti, where their red bean is called *congó* and rice is *riz*, just like the French. *Congrí* then is a diminutive of *congós* with rice. Versions across the island include sausage, chorizo and even chickpeas. If you ask me for *arroz congrí*, I can assure you I will serve you *Moros y Cristianos* (page 121). Interestingly, this recipe is almost the same, with detectable differences in the flavor profile the beans are responsible for offering.

This dish pairs extremely well with the *Carne con Papa* (page 53).

SERVES 6

5½ cups (1.3 L) water

1½ cups (300 g) dried light or dark small red beans, picked through and rinsed

1 bay leaf

¼ cup (60 ml) vegetable oil

1 medium yellow onion, diced

1 green bell pepper, diced

5 cloves garlic, finely pressed

1½ tsp (9 g) kosher salt

2 cups (391 g) uncooked long-grain white rice

1 tbsp (15 ml) olive oil

Add the water, red beans and bay leaf to the cooker. Close the lid.

Stovetop: Set to high pressure (15 PSI) and set the timer for 30 minutes total. Cook over high heat until the pressure point is reached, then lower the heat to medium and continue to cook.

Electric: Use the bean setting, or set to high pressure (10–12 PSI) and 30 minutes.

While the beans are cooking, make the *sofrito*: In a medium skillet, heat the vegetable oil and sauté the onion, bell pepper and garlic, stirring until the onion is translucent and the flavors marry well, about 3 to 4 minutes. Remove from the heat.

When the beans are done, turn off the heat or cancel cooking and release the pressure, using auto-release for the stovetop cooker or slow auto-release for the electric cooker (refer to page 20 if needed). When all of the pressure is out, open the cooker and add the *sofrito*. Season with the salt and stir. Bring to a boil, for the stovetop pressure cooker, or use the sauté setting for the electric pressure cooker, about 3 to 4 minutes. For the stovetop cooker, lower the heat to medium, or cancel cooking for the electric cooker. Stir in the rice and close the lid.

Stovetop: Set to high pressure (15 PSI) and cook over medium heat for 15 minutes total.

Electric: Use the rice setting, or set to low pressure (5–8 PSI) and 20 minutes.

When done, turn off the heat or turn off the cooker and release the pressure, using auto-release for the stovetop cooker or slow auto-release for the electric cooker. When all of the pressure is out, open the cooker and drizzle with the olive oil. Gently separate and fluff the rice grains, using a fork, working your way to the bottom of the cooker. Serve hot.

A portion of my spice and dried herb collection.

"MOORS AND CHRISTIANS," A.K.A. BLACK BEAN RICE

"Moros y Cristianos" o Arroz Congrí

This is the most ironic dish of Cuba. Aptly named to reflect the two fighting groups, the Moors and the Christians, it turns out to be a perfect and inseparable marriage between two of Cuba's most eaten foods. Its popularity makes the pressure cooker an essential tool in homes. Cooking dried beans for three to four hours is not very appealing when you know it can be done in 45 minutes. In all its simplicity, it's quite lovely. Also, try making the garlic confit. It's magic! This dish pairs extremely well with my Pulled Flank Steak in Red Wine Sauce recipe (page 127).

SERVES 5 TO 6

5 cups (1.2 L) water or Simple Vegetable Broth (page 157)

1½ cups (375 g) dried black beans, picked through and rinsed

1 bay leaf

¼ cup (60 ml) vegetable oil

1 medium yellow onion, diced

1 Cubanelle pepper, diced

5 cloves garlic, finely pressed and 3 mashed (optional)

1 tsp (6 g) kosher salt

2 cups (388 g) uncooked long-grain white rice

1 tbsp (15 ml) olive oil

Add the water or vegetable broth, black beans and bay leaf to the cooker. Close the lid.

Stovetop: Set to high pressure (15 PSI) and set the timer for 25 minutes total. Cook over high heat until the pressure point is reached, then lower the heat to medium or enough to maintain pressure and continue to cook.

Electric: Set to high pressure (10–12 PSI) and 25 minutes.

While the beans are cooking, make the *sofrito*: In a medium skillet, heat the vegetable oil and sauté the onion, Cubanelle pepper and garlic, stirring until the onion is translucent and the flavors marry well, about 4 minutes. Remove from the heat.

When the beans are done, turn off the heat or cancel cooking and release the pressure, using auto-release for the stovetop cooker or slow auto-release for the electric cooker (refer to page 20 if needed). When all of the pressure is out, open the cooker and add the *sofrito*. Season with the salt and stir. Stir in the rice and close the lid.

Stovetop: Set to high pressure (15 PSI) and cook over medium-high heat for 12 minutes total.

Electric: Use the rice setting, or set to low pressure (5–8 PSI) and 12 minutes.

When done, turn off the heat or turn off the cooker and release the pressure, using auto-release. When all of the pressure is out, open the cooker and drizzle with olive oil. Gently separate and fluff the rice grains, using a fork, working your way to the bottom of the cooker. If you'd like, heat the remaining olive oil and quickly brown the 3 cloves of mashed garlic. Drizzle it all over the rice before serving. The smell is intense and the added layer of flavor and texture is divine.

Serve hot.

Hearty Red Beans and Squash Stew

Potaje de Frijoles Colorado

Red beans are my Mami's second-favorite bean and therefore cooked much more than any other. This dish is so hearty, so filling and so rustic. The butternut squash isn't typical but adds some sweetness to the beans. It's a beautiful *potaje* that demonstrates how much you love your loved ones. Much like the other bean stews, you can add a meat of your choice for added depth and flavor.

Serves 6 to 8

2 cups (400 g) dried red beans, picked through and rinsed

1 bay leaf

8½ cups (2.1 L) water, divided

¼ cup (60 ml) canola oil

1 medium Vidalia onion, diced

4 cloves garlic, mashed and minced

½ green bell pepper, diced

1 tsp (2.5 g) ground cumin

1 tbsp (3 g) dried oregano

¼ cup (60 ml) tomato sauce

1 cup (140 g) seeded and cubed butternut squash (1½" [4-cm] cubes)

1 large potato, peeled and cut into 1" (2.5-cm) cubes

1 tbsp (18 g) kosher salt

Add the beans, bay leaf and 6 cups (1.4 L) of the water to the cooker. Close the lid.

Stovetop: Set to high pressure (15 PSI) and set the timer for 35 minutes. Cook over high heat until the pressure point is reached, then lower the heat to medium and continue to cook.

Electric: Set to high pressure (10–12 PSI) and 35 minutes.

When done, turn off the heat or cancel cooking and release the pressure, using auto-release.

While the pressure is releasing, make the *sofrito*: In a medium skillet over medium-high heat, heat the oil and sauté the onions, garlic and bell pepper until fragrant, adding the cumin and oregano, about 3 minutes. Lower the heat and stir in the tomato sauce.

When all of the pressure is out, open the cooker. Using the back of a wooden spoon, gently mash the beans against the cooker, only enough to create a bit more density. Add the remaining 2½ cups (590 ml) of water to the cooker. Stir in the *sofrito*, butternut squash and potato, scraping everything from the skillet with a spatula. Season with the salt and close the lid.

Stovetop: Set to low pressure (8 PSI) and cook over high heat for 8 minutes total.

Electric: Set to low pressure (5–8 PSI) and 8 minutes.

When done, remove from the heat or turn off the cooker and allow the pressure to release on its own (natural-release), about 10 minutes. If you can find it, remove the bay leaf.

Serve hot over fluffy white rice. This can also be enjoyed on its own as a really hearty "soup." If you prefer that, add an additional cup (235 ml) of water or Simple Vegetable Broth (page 157) and let simmer for 10 minutes, uncovered.

CHICKPEA AND BEEF TRIPE STEW

Garbanzos con Panza

Offal, including organ meats, is becoming increasingly popular in America and is seen more and more on avant-garde menus. Still, some people are unsure how it tastes and think the texture is a bit odd. Until this trendy wave, not knowing how to cook certain parts of the cow has kept most of them at bay. I'll tell you tripe is my favorite offal. I'm thankful my mother introduced me to it at an early age. There's nothing odd about it and can be a great surprise to certain dishes needing an extra element. This version of chickpea stew is known more in the countryside of the island where the "cheaper" parts of the cow are common. I omitted the *pata*, or cow's feet, and let the honeycomb tripe speak volumes. I also don't want to scare you off with too many offal in one dish! The tripe has an amazing texture and adds a unique flavor. I also consolidated the process to highlight the benefits of pressure-cooking. Tripe can take over one hour to tenderize. In this dish, it's done in 30 minutes.

SERVES 6 TO 8

3½ cups (828 ml) water

1 lb (455 g) honeycomb tripe, rinsed thoroughly and cut into 1½" to 2" (4- to 5-cm) pieces

4 cloves garlic, minced, divided

2 medium bay leaves

2 tsp (12 g) kosher salt

3 tbsp (45 ml) canola oil

½ Spanish onion, diced

½ red bell pepper, diced

½ tsp ground cumin

2 tsp (2 g) dried oregano

1 packet Sazón seasoning (without achiote, optional)

3 (15-oz [425-g]) cans chickpeas, drained and rinsed

2 tbsp (32 g) tomato paste

1 potato, skin on and cubed

2 tsp (10 ml) olive oil

Add the water, tripe, half of the garlic, the bay leaves and salt to the cooker. Stir and close the lid.

Stovetop: Set to high pressure (15 PSI) and cook over high heat for 40 minutes total. When the pressure point has been reached, reduce the heat to medium-high or enough to maintain high pressure. I typically keep it at high the first 30 minutes.

Electric: Set to high pressure (10–12 PSI) and 45 minutes.

When done, remove from the heat or cancel cooking and release the pressure, using slow auto-release (refer to page 19 if needed), about 10 minutes.

While the pressure is releasing, make the *sofrito*: Heat the canola oil in a medium skillet. Sauté the onion, bell pepper, remaining garlic, cumin, oregano and Sazón, about 4 minutes. Add the *sofrito*, chickpeas, tomato paste and potato to the cooker. Gently mash the chickpeas against the wall of the cooker, using the back of a wooden spoon. Close the lid.

Stovetop: Set to high pressure (15 PSI) and set the timer for 8 minutes. Cook over high heat until the pressure is reached, then lower the heat to medium and continue to cook.

Electric: Set to high pressure (10–12 PSI) and 10 minutes.

When done, remove the stovetop pressure cooker from the heat and release the pressure, using auto-release. Open the cooker and drizzle in the olive oil. Adjust for salt. Allow the chickpeas to sit for 5 minutes, uncovered. Discard the bay leaves before serving.

BEST YOU'VE EVER HAD BRAISED ROUND ROAST

Carne Asada o Boliche

If there's one single beef dish that could convert a slow cooker enthusiast to pressure-cooking, this would be it. Cooking times for quality top round can be upward of two and a half to three hours. This family recipe has been the same for over 20 years and always delights with high compliments, from home cooks to 20-year executive chef authorities. The gravy is elegantly rich but not overpowering, a direct result of braising. It's also all about the *mojo criollo*, or the liquid marinade, which recipe I include below.

SERVES 6

2½ lb (1.1 kg) top round beef

8 cloves garlic, mashed, divided

1 tsp (2.5 g) ground cumin

1 tbsp (3 g) dried oregano

1 tsp (6 g) kosher salt

¼ cup (60 ml) white distilled vinegar

¼ cup (60 ml) dry white cooking wine

⅓ cup (80 ml) vegetable oil

3 cups (710 ml) dry red wine

B'S COOKING TIP: This dish is best served with a carb or side that will absorb the *jus* really well. I suggest white rice or creamy mashed potatoes. Alternatively, serve with a simple side of *haricots verts* and roasted French carrots.

Wash and trim the excess fat off the beef. Pat dry and place in a deep pan or dish for seasoning. Using a paring knife, lightly score the beef on top, creating 1-inch (2.5-cm) deep cuts. Stuff those slits with half of the garlic. In a processor or blender, process the remaining garlic, cumin, oregano, salt, vinegar and white cooking wine until well blended, about 1 minute. This is the *mojo*, or seasoning marinade. Cover the entire roast with the marinade, stuffing the slits with it. Cover and chill for 2 hours. This chilling process is not completely necessary but will highly impact the resulting flavor.

Heat the stovetop pressure cooker over high, or use the browning setting for the electric pressure cooker, then add the oil. Using only sturdy tongs, transfer only the roast to the pressure cooker and brown on all sides, until very golden but not burned, turning only once, about 8 minutes total, reducing the heat to medium-high at the halfway point. Cancel cooking with 3 minutes remaining for the electric cooker. Add the *mojo* and coat the roast. Pour in the red wine, covering the roast. Close the lid.

Stovetop: Set to high pressure (15 PSI) and set the timer for 30 minutes. Cook over high heat until the pressure point has been reached, then lower the heat to medium and continue to cook.

Electric: Set to high pressure (10–12 PSI) and 35 minutes.

When done, remove from the heat or turn off the cooker and allow the pressure to release on its own (natural-release). When all of the pressure is out, open the cooker and transfer the roast to a carving board.

Return the stovetop pressure cooker to the stove and reduce the sauce over medium heat, or set the electric cooker to the simmer function, for 6 to 10 minutes. Slice the roast crosswise into 1½-inch (4-cm) slices. Transfer to a serving dish. Ladle the reduced browned *jus* over the roast, covering it all.

Pulled Flank Steak in Red Wine Sauce

Ropa Vieja o Carne Ripiada

I'm excited for you to try this robust shredded beef dish, which literally translates to "old clothes" or "old, shredded clothes." Pressure cooking a 1½-pound (680-g) flank steak makes shredding this lean meat really easy. The red wine makes the sauce very round but I've also used white cooking wine, defying classical pairing trends, and it works just as lovely. That's the beauty of making food your own. There's nothing else like this classic Cuban recipe. President Obama enjoyed this very dish during his historical visit to Havana in spring 2016. We traditionally eat this rice with *Moros y Cristianos* (page 121). The sauce is also lovely over vegetables, or any rice.

Serves 6

3 cups (710 ml) water

1½ lb (680 g) flank steak

2 bay leaves

1 tbsp (18 g) plus 2 tsp (12 g) kosher salt

⅓ cup (80 ml) canola oil

1 medium Spanish onion, cut into ½" (1.3-cm) julienne

1 medium green bell pepper, cut into ½" (1.3-cm) julienne

1 medium red bell pepper, cut into ½" (1.3-cm) julienne

4 cloves garlic, minced

1 tsp (1 g) dried oregano

½ tsp ground cumin

1 cup (245 g) tomato sauce

1 cup (235 ml) dry red wine

1 tbsp (15 ml) white distilled vinegar

⅛ tsp freshly ground black pepper

Add the water, flank steak and bay leaves to the cooker. Season with 1 tablespoon (18 g) of the salt. Close the lid.

Stovetop: Set to high pressure (15 PSI) and set the timer for 30 minutes. Cook over high heat until the pressure point is reached, then lower the heat to medium and continue to cook.

Electric: Use the meat setting and adjust the time to 35 minutes, or set to high pressure (10–12 PSI) and 35 minutes.

When done, remove the stovetop cooker from the heat and apply quick-release, or cancel cooking for the electric cooker and apply auto-release. When all the pressure is out, open the cooker and transfer the flank steak to a carving board, using tongs. Allow the beef to rest, about 5 minutes. Reserve 1 cup (235 ml) of the beef stock for later use and discard the rest. Do not discard the bay leaves. When ready, manually shred the beef, pulling it apart into ½-inch (1.3-cm) wide pieces. Heat the oil in the stovetop pressure cooker over medium-high or use the sauté setting for the electric pressure cooker. Sauté all of the vegetables and garlic, adding the oregano and cumin, until the onion begins to soften and the mixture is fragrant, about 2 to 5 minutes. Stir in the tomato sauce, red wine and reserved beef stock. Add the shredded beef, vinegar and black pepper, and adjust for salt. Stir well, cancel cooking for the electric cooker and close the lid.

Stovetop: Set to high pressure (15 PSI) and cook over high heat for 10 minutes total.

Electric: Use the meat setting and adjust the time to 15 minutes, or set to high pressure (10–12 PSI) and 15 minutes.

When done, remove from the heat or turn off the cooker and allow the pressure to release on its own (natural-release), about 7 to 10 minutes. If the pressure is not fully released after 10 minutes, apply auto-release. Serve immediately.

Chicken Fricassee

Pollo en Fricasé

Of all of the recipes in this cookbook, this is my most special. There are at least eight versions I know of, the oldest I'm aware of dating back to the early 1900s. It was my default recipe when entertaining in my early 20s. None of my friends at the time was familiar with Cuban food, so this was always a huge hit. It's also the first recipe I ever shared with anyone. It's a perfectly balanced sweet and savory chicken that shines in every bite. You'll be remarkably impressed with the results in just 15 minutes. The chicken is succulent and extremely tender, much juicier than you can imagine. As most things go with our food, this is best enjoyed with white rice and a fresh green salad. I always fry sweet plantains, too.

Serves 6

2 lb (905 g) chicken (4 breasts, 4 legs)

2 tbsp (36 g) kosher salt

¼ tsp freshly ground black pepper

1 tbsp (15 ml) canola oil

1 bay leaf

¼ tsp ground cumin

½ tsp dried oregano

1 cup (160 g) white onion, diced

1 green bell pepper, cut into ½" (1.3-cm) julienne

5 cloves garlic, mashed

3 tbsp (45 ml) white distilled vinegar

1 cup (245 g) tomato sauce

2 large carrots, cut into 1" (2.5-cm) round slices

1½ tsp (4 g) capers, rinsed

½ cup (50 g) Spanish olives with pimiento

½ cup (120 ml) dry white cooking wine

½ cup (120 ml) red wine

2 white potatoes, cut into 1" (2.5-cm) pieces

¼ cup (35 g) raisins

Season the chicken with the salt and black pepper. Heat the stovetop pressure cooker over medium-high or use the browning setting for the electric pressure cooker, and add the oil. Add the chicken and lightly brown on all sides, about 3 minutes. Add the bay leaf, cumin, oregano, onion, bell pepper, garlic and vinegar and stir. For the stovetop pressure cooker, reduce the heat to medium and cook for 2 minutes, then lower the heat to medium-low and maintain as you are incorporating ingredients; for the electric pressure cooker, cancel the browning setting. Add the remaining ingredients in the order listed, then cook over low heat for the stovetop cooker, or using the residual heat for the electric cooker, for 5 minutes, stirring very gently, making sure not to tear the chicken. Close the lid.

Stovetop: Set to high pressure (15 PSI) and set the timer for 15 minutes. Cook over high heat until the pressure point is reached, then lower the heat to medium and continue to cook.

Electric: Use the meat setting and adjust the time to 20 minutes, or set to high pressure (10–12 PSI) and 20 minutes.

When done, remove from the heat or turn off the cooker and release the pressure, using auto-release. When all of the pressure it out, open the cooker, adjust for salt and serve.

CLASSIC CHICKPEA STEW WITH CHORIZO

Potaje de Garbanzos con Chorizo

I've been on a mission to introduce chickpeas to anyone who will entertain my affection. It's not as common in American cuisine—possibly because of their hardness and lengthy cooking time—but often enjoyed in Latin America, the Middle East and India, in a wide variety of dishes, from spicy stews to creamy falafel to hummus. In Cuba, chickpeas are enjoyed as a really soulful stew, usually amplified with potatoes and butternut squash. This one-hour version is one my parents reserve for fall and winter months. I like to enjoy it whenever, even cheating with canned chickpeas. The chorizo brings it all together, but try other smoky meats if you're not into pork.

SERVES 8 TO 10

½ gallon (1.9 L) plus 1 cup (235 ml) water or Herbed Chicken Stock (page 166)

14 oz (400 g) dried chickpeas, picked through and rinsed *2 cups*

1 tbsp (18 g) salt, or to taste

2 bay leaves

3 tbsp (45 ml) canola oil

1 large Spanish onion, cut into medium dice

1 green bell pepper, cut into medium dice

5 garlic cloves, minced

1 tsp (1 g) dried oregano

½ tsp ground cumin

1 (1-tsp [5-g]) packet Sazón (without achiote) or your own spice blend

8 oz (225 g) tomato sauce

1 chorizo, cut into 4 (1" [2.5-cm]) pieces

2 red potatoes, peeled and cubed into 1½" (4-cm) cubes

1 cup (140 g) seeded and cubed butternut squash (1" [2.5-cm] cubes)

2 tsp (10 ml) olive oil

Add all the water or chicken stock, chickpeas, salt and bay leaves to the cooker. Stir and close the lid.

Stovetop: Set to high pressure (15 PSI) and cook over high heat for 25 minutes total.

Electric: Set to high pressure (10–12 PSI) and 35 minutes.

While the chickpeas are cooking, make the *sofrito*: Heat the canola oil in a medium skillet. Sauté the onion, bell pepper, garlic and all of the remaining dried seasonings over medium heat until the onion begins to soften, about 4 minutes. Turn off the heat and set aside.

When the chickpeas are done, remove the stovetop cooker from the heat and apply a quick-release, or cancel cooking for the electric cooker and apply auto-release. When all of the pressure is out, open the cooker and stir in the tomato sauce. Add the *sofrito*, chorizo, potatoes and squash. Stir well, using the back of the wooden spoon to gently mash the chickpeas. This will provide some added density. Close the lid.

Stovetop: Set to high pressure (15 PSI) and set the timer for 25 minutes. Cook over high heat until the pressure point is reached, then lower the heat to medium and continue to cook.

Electric: Use the stew setting, or set to high pressure (10–12 PSI) and 30 minutes.

When done, remove from the heat or turn off the cooker and allow the pressure to release on its own (natural-release), about 8 to 10 minutes. If the pressure has not been fully released after 10 minutes, apply auto-release. Open the cooker and slowly drizzle in the olive oil. Adjust for salt. Allow the chickpeas to sit for 5 minutes, uncovered. Discard the bay leaves before serving.

Serve with fluffy white rice.

EASY TIME-SAVER STAPLES
Meals Under 30 Minutes

The dishes in this chapter will marry you to pressure cooking for the rest of your life, if the other recipes in the book haven't done so already! If you're ever short on time and creativity, these options are varied in both protein and carbohydrates, allowing you to create full dinners. My point here is to give you a few ideas that illustrate how practical pressure cooking is without losing any of the nutritional benefits. Some are a bit more complex in flavor than others, but they're all done in a snap. Check out the 10-Minute Black Beans (page 137); they are my simplified version of the dried beans recipe and offer flexibility in what you pair them with. They are so easy to make and turn into a hearty lunch or quick, simple dinner for the family. The Savory Eggplant and Potato Mélange (page 146) is rustic and romantic at the same time. Its earthiness connects you to the source of good nutrition. The variety in flavor throughout the recipes is wonderful for you to explore; it offers something different when you're in a hurry for good food.

15-Minute Creole Kidney Beans and Chorizo

This smoky rice turned out to be a combination a southern-food lover will enjoy. I've been on a serious smoked paprika kick and am loving finding more and more dishes to which I can add a pinch here and there. You might walk away wanting to host a campfire when you smell the combination of the smoked paprika with the smoked chorizo. It's a twist on celebrating Spanish ingredients with southern tradition. What I really created is a delicious cheat to the original *Arroz Congrí* (page 117) and it proves to be an inviting lunch option any day of the week. Eat this with steamed cabbage and other vegetables.

SERVES 6

3 tbsp (45 ml) olive oil

½ cup (80 g) diced red onion

½ cup (75 g) diced red bell pepper

2 cloves garlic, minced

1 bay leaf

1 smoked chorizo or Andouille sausage, sliced

1 tbsp (7 g) smoked paprika

2 tsp (10 ml) Worcestershire sauce

2 cups (380 g) uncooked white rice

1 (16-oz [455-g]) can dark kidney beans, undrained

2½ cups (590 ml) water or Simple Vegetable Broth (page 157)

2 tsp (12 g) salt

Heat the olive oil in the stovetop pressure cooker over medium or use the sauté function for the electric pressure cooker. Make the *sofrito*: Sauté the onion, bell pepper, garlic and bay leaf until the onion is softened, about 2 minutes. Add the sausage, paprika and Worcestershire sauce. Reduce the heat to medium-low for the stovetop cooker or cancel cooking for the electric cooker, stirring until all of the ingredients are well blended. Add the rice, kidney beans, water or vegetable broth and salt, in that order, and stir. Close the lid.

Stovetop: Set to low pressure (8 PSI) and cook over high heat for 10 minutes total.

Electric: Use the rice setting, or set to low pressure (5–8 PSI) and 10 minutes.

When done, remove from the heat or turn off the cooker and release the pressure, using slow auto-release (refer to page 19 if needed). When all of the pressure is out, open the cooker and fluff the rice, separating the grains, using a fork.

 B'S COOKING TIP: If you have only one setting on your stovetop pressure cooker, cook over medium heat for 13 minutes.

ULTRACREAMY MALANGA

My mother would be considered a modern-day "helicopter mom." She was into everything my siblings and I did growing up. Taking care of us was her priority, as for any other mother. When we were sick, the first thing she'd make for us, especially me and my youngest brother, was *purée de malanga*, a supercreamy mash of a chunky and rustic root vegetable, fluffed with some milk and sometimes a drizzle of olive oil. There was nothing more. I loved it so much, I probably used to pretend to be sick just so she would make some. Malanga is a root tuber indigenous to South America and somewhat similar to taro. It's much healthier than the potato but prepared in similar ways. A simple purée can replace mashed potatoes and be whipped up in just ten minutes in the pressure cooker.

SERVES 6

2½ lb (1.1 kg) fresh malanga or taro root, peeled and cut in 2" (5-cm) chunks

2 cups (475 ml) water

1 tsp (6 g) coarse salt

2 tbsp (28 ml) olive oil

5 cloves garlic, finely minced

1 cup (235 ml) milk

1 tbsp (14 g) unsalted butter

¼ cup (60 g) sliced spring onion

Add the malanga, water and salt to the pressure cooker. Close the lid.

Stovetop: Set to high pressure (15 PSI) and cook over high heat for 10 minutes total.

Electric: Set to high pressure (10–12 PSI) and 12 minutes.

When done, remove from the heat or turn off the cooker and release the pressure, using auto-release.

While the pressure is releasing, brown the garlic: Add the olive oil to a small skillet and brown the garlic evenly, stirring gently, about 1 minute. Be careful not to burn it.

When all of the pressure is out, open the cooker and fold in the milk, garlic with its excess olive oil and the butter, in that order. Mash the malanga, using a potato masher, until all the pieces are broken down and ultracreamy. Stir in the spring onion.

Adjust for salt, if desired. Serve immediately.

 B IN THE KNOW! Malanga comes only as the fresh root. I've never been able to find it frozen like yuca. However, you can find it in most international food markets; depending on where you live, some national chain markets will have it in the produce section.

 B'S COOKING TIP: The starch in this root tuber will cause it to harden rather fast. To soften, whip in warm milk or cream and stir.

10-Minute Black Beans

This is the express version of the already-fast Famous Cuban Black Beans (page 72). Canned beans need some flavor but the time savings are ideal for the really busy person not wanting to sacrifice good food. You can add simple meats, such as chorizo, kielbasa (turkey, chicken or pork) or other sausage for added volume and flavor. You can enjoy this over rice or on its own.

Serves 4

3 tbsp (45 ml) canola oil

½ cup (80 g) diced white onion

½ orange bell pepper, diced

3 cloves garlic, minced

1 tsp (3 g) small-diced jalapeño pepper

1 bay leaf

⅛ tsp ground cumin

⅛ tsp ground nutmeg

⅛ tsp paprika

⅛ tsp freshly ground black pepper

1½ tsp (6 g) sugar

1 (16-oz [455-g]) can black beans

2 cups (475 ml) water or Simple Vegetable Broth (page 157)

6 sprigs flat-leaf parsley

Salt

Heat the oil in the stovetop pressure cooker over high or use the sauté function for the electric pressure cooker and make the *sofrito*: Sauté the onion, bell pepper, garlic and jalapeño until the onion is translucent, about 2 minutes. Add the remaining ingredients in the order listed, seasoning with salt to taste, and stir. Cancel cooking for the electric cooker, and close the lid.

Stovetop: Set to high pressure (15 PSI) and cook over high heat for 8 minutes total.

Electric: Set to high pressure (10–12 PSI) and 10 minutes.

When done, remove from the heat or turn off the cooker and release the pressure, using auto-release. Adjust for salt. Garnish with additional parsley, if desired.

Serve immediately.

 B CREATIVE! You can also enjoy this cold on a really hot day, kind of like a gazpacho. Allow it to chill for about 2 hours, then process in a blender, adding 2 to 3 plum tomatoes and 2 additional garlic cloves. Blend for about 3 minutes until you have a textured consistency.

CREAMY POTATO SALAD

Off the top of my head I can think of eight different potatoes you can use to make potato salad. Some are milder than others. Others are more buttery. For this recipe, I like using the most buttery potato I've ever come across, called Rooster potatoes. They add a great amount of natural creaminess to the salad. You can offer to take a bright potato salad to every cookout, summer party or family reunion, knowing all you need is 20 or so minutes, total, prep to finish.

SERVES 10 TO 12

2½ lb (1.1 kg) white potatoes, washed and cut into 1½" (4-cm) chunks

1½ cups (355 ml) water

1½ tsp (9 g) salt

4 cloves garlic, mashed

1 cup (225 g) good mayonnaise

¼ cup (44 g) whole-grain Dijon mustard

1 cup (100 g) diced celery (medium dice)

1 cup (100 g) Spanish olives, pitted and halved lengthwise

¼ cup (12 g) thinly sliced fresh chives

1 tsp (2 g) freshly ground black pepper

1 tsp (2.5 g) smoked paprika, plus a little more as desired

2 large eggs, cooked and sliced into quarter moons (optional)

¼ cup (12 g) chives, chopped

Fresh cilantro, for garnish

Add the potatoes, water and salt to the cooker. Close the lid.

Stovetop: Set to high pressure (15 PSI) and cook over high heat for 10 minutes total.

Electric: Set to high pressure (10–12 PSI) and 11 minutes.

When done, remove from the heat or turn off the cooker and release the pressure, using auto-release. When all of the pressure is out, open the cooker and allow the potatoes to cool, about 5 minutes. Drain the water, using a colander, and transfer the potatoes, along with the garlic, to a large mixing bowl. Gently fold in the mayonnaise and mustard, using a rubber or silicone spatula. Add the celery, olives, chives, black pepper, paprika and cooked eggs, if using. Gently stir again until all of the ingredients are well combined. Adjust for salt. Refrigerate until ready to serve. Garnish with the cilantro, chives and a dash more of smoked paprika.

 B'S COOKING TIP: Replace the Dijon mustard with the same amount of tarragon mustard featured in the Tarragon-Mustard Braised Short Ribs recipe on page 56. It's a beautiful twist.

CLASSIC RAGOUT

This is a classic French sauce used over the top of starchy foods, such as rice, potatoes or pastas, meat dishes and a myriad of other foods. There are thousands of interpretations inspired by region, trend and diet. I love my version for its robust use of herbs. I also appreciate the intensity of the garlic. My favorite base has been orzo. Also, a packet of Sazón is optional here if you're looking for a bit more flavor.

SERVES 6

¼ cup (60 ml) olive oil

1 cup (160 g) diced Vidalia onion

8 garlic cloves, minced

1 stalk celery, finely diced

2 bay leaves

1 tbsp (7.5 g) all-purpose flour

½ cup (118 ml) Herbed Beef Stock
(page 167), or store-bought

3 beefsteak tomatoes, peeled and quartered

2 tbsp (32 g) tomato paste

Leaves from 13 sprigs curly parsley, chopped

3 sprigs fresh basil, finely chopped

1 cup (235 ml) dry red wine

1½ tsp (1.5 g) dried oregano

½ tsp ground cumin

¼ tsp freshly ground black pepper

1½ tsp (9 g) kosher salt

1 tsp (4.5 g) sugar

Heat the olive oil in the stovetop pressure cooker over low or use the soup setting for the electric pressure cooker. Sweat the onion with the garlic, celery and bay leaf until the onion is softened, 3 to 4 minutes. Whisk in the flour and stir until all of the clumps are gone. Add the beef stock and cook for 3 minutes over low heat for the stovetop pressure cooker or cancel the soup setting for the electric pressure cooker. Add all of the remaining ingredients. Mash the tomatoes, using a potato masher, until most are broken down. Close the lid.

Stovetop: Set to high pressure (15 PSI) and cook over high heat for 7 minutes total.

Electric: Set to high pressure (10–12 PSI) and 9 minutes.

When done, remove from the heat or turn off the cooker and allow the pressure to release on its own (natural-release), about 3 to 5 minutes. When all of the pressure is out, open the cooker. Stir and adjust for salt, if necessary, and serve. This is ideal to use in pasta sauces, either meat or vegetarian.

SMOKY COLOMBIAN SAUSAGE RAGOUT

You really can't go wrong with a bold ragout for your favorite carbs. It's almost effortless cooking that provides plenty of options. I love that you can double and triple this recipe for larger feedings or because you need to have extra for those lazy, über-busy days. The plantain in this smoky version is just what you'll be talking about. Feel free to replace the quinoa with any of your other favorite grains or pasta.

SERVES 6

2 lb (905 g) Colombian smoked sausage, sliced in into ½" (1.3-cm) slices

1 tbsp (16 g) tomato paste

10 oz (280 g) carrots, peeled and cut into ½" (1.3-cm) cubes

2 cups (320 g) peeled and chopped Spanish onion

5 cloves garlic, finely chopped

1 cup (150 g) chopped red bell pepper

1 green plantain, peeled, cut into ½" (1.3-cm) cubes

1 tbsp (18 g) kosher salt

2 dried bay leaves

¼ tsp ground thyme

¼ tsp fennel seeds

½ tsp ground cumin

2 tbsp (3 g) ground dried cilantro

2½ cups (590 ml) Herbed Chicken Stock (page 166), or store-bought

1½ cups (255 g) uncooked quinoa, rinsed

Heat the stovetop pressure cooker over high or use the browning setting for the electric pressure cooker. Add the Colombian sausage to brown, about 3 minutes. Remove the sausage from the pressure cooker and set aside. Add all of the remaining ingredients, except the chicken stock and quinoa, and sauté over medium-high heat for the stovetop cooker or maintain the browning setting for the electric cooker, about 2 minutes. Add the sausage, chicken stock and quinoa and stir to incorporate all the ingredients. Cancel cooking for the electric cooker, and close the lid.

Stovetop: Set to low pressure (8 PSI) and cook over high heat for 20 minutes total.

Electric: Use the soup/stew setting, or set to low pressure (5–8 PSI) and 20 minutes.

When done, remove from the heat or turn off the cooker and release the pressure, using auto-release. Serve immediately over your favorite starch or roasted vegetables.

WARM BUTTERNUT SQUASH AND PISTACHIO PURÉE

This winter squash is so versatile it's hard to avoid. It's possibly my favorite of the wide range in pumpkins and squash. The short cooking time in the pressure cooker easily invites it to many other dishes. I love the buttery texture and the pistachios add a fantastic element of surprise. Sometimes, this will be all you need to satisfy sweet and savory cravings.

SERVES 4

¼ cup (26 g) whole pistachios, plus more for garnish

1 medium butternut squash, peeled, seeded and cut into 2" (5-cm) pieces

1 tsp (6 g) kosher salt

¼ cup (60 g) packed light brown sugar

1 cup (235 ml) water

1 tsp (1 g) ground dried sage

1 tbsp (14 g) butter

Dark brown sugar or agave nectar (optional)

Fresh micro sage leaves, for garnish

Using a mortar, crush the pistachios until really ground, almost becoming a lightly textured powder but not fully pulverized. If you don't have a mortar and pestle, pulse in a mini food processor until the pistachios are crushed and ground but not pulverized. Add all of the ingredients to the pressure cooker, except the butter and optional sweetener. Close the lid.

Stovetop: Set to high pressure (15 PSI) and cook over high heat for 6 minutes total.

Electric: Set to high pressure (10–12 PSI) and 8 minutes.

When done, remove from the heat or turn off the cooker and allow the pressure to release on its own (natural-release). When all of the pressure is out, about 8 minutes, open the cooker and whip in the butter. Mash the squash with a potato masher until all of the clumps are broken down. Blend all of the ingredients well, using a wooden spoon.

Sweeten with agave or brown sugar, if desired. Adjust the salt. Garnish with chunkier pieces of crushed pistachio and fresh sage leaves.

Serve this as a side with chicken or a juicy steak.

 B'S COOKING TIP: Toast the pistachios for a more nutty flavor and aroma. Simply cook in a small amount of butter or olive oil in a small skillet until they are evenly toasty, about 3 minutes.

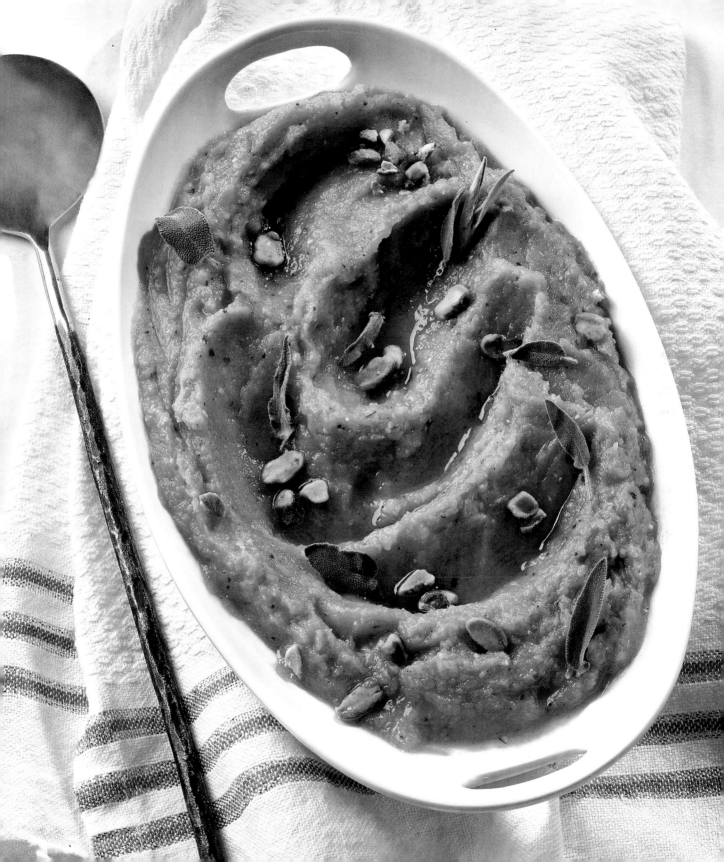

Soulful Beef, Okra and Plantain Mélange

Peasant dishes have a way of evolving and lingering through generations. I had never enjoyed this robust duo of vegetables and beef until recently and was intrigued by the pairing of "green" plantain and okra, two opposites that attract. However, a very similar combination is common in West African cuisine, as I've come to find out. Add more culture and global flair to your cooking experience with this hearty mélange.

Serves 4 to 6

1½ cups (355 ml) water

½ cup (120 ml) freshly squeezed lemon juice

1 lb (455 g) fresh okra, rinsed and dried

1 tbsp (15 ml) extra-virgin olive oil

½ Vidalia onion, chopped

½ green or red bell pepper, chopped

5 cloves garlic, minced

1 tsp (1 g) dried oregano

¼ tsp ground cumin

2 lb (905 g) sirloin, sliced into 1½" (4-cm) pieces

1 tsp (6 g) kosher salt

½ tsp cayenne pepper

½ tsp freshly ground black pepper

1 midripe plantain, cut into 1" (2.5-cm) pieces

½ cup (123 g) tomato sauce

2 cups (475 ml) Herbed Beef Stock (page 167), or store-bought

1 cup (235 ml) dry red cooking wine

1 tbsp (15 ml) white distilled vinegar

Add the water and lemon juice to a medium bowl. Soak the okra and gently wash to reduce its slimy texture. Drain and pat dry. Heat the oil in the stovetop pressure cooker over medium-low or use the low pressure function for the electric pressure cooker. Sweat the onion, bell pepper and garlic, about 2 minutes. Season with the oregano and cumin. Add the beef and season with the salt, cayenne and black pepper. Brown the meat for 2 minutes over high heat or cancel cooking and reset to the sauté setting for the electric cooker. Lower the heat of the stovetop pressure cooker to medium-high, or cancel cooking for the electric cooker. Add the okra and plantain and stir. Pour in the tomato sauce, beef stock, cooking wine and vinegar. Stir well to combine the ingredients and close the lid.

Stovetop: Set to high pressure (15 PSI) and cook over medium-high heat for 12 minutes total.

Electric: Set to high pressure (10–12 PSI) and 15 minutes.

When done, remove from the heat or turn off the cooker and allow the pressure to release on its own (natural-release), about 8 minutes. When all of the pressure is out, open the cooker, stir and adjust for salt. Serve as a lovely savory topping to a rustic bowl of Creamy Corn Polenta (plain, without the canned or fresh corn; page 38).

B'S COOKING TIP: It's key to use a midripe plantain for this dish. A ripe plantain will be too sweet and will break down to a soft texture and make the dish sweet and mushy. Look for one with a mostly green hue with minor yellow spots. See the plantain chart on page 34 for reference.

Savory Eggplant and Potato Mélange

It is no secret among my closest friends and family that my precious mother and I have two completely different styles in the kitchen. She's very methodical, needing to be in complete control of modifications. I like to allow my mood and base food to inspire my creativity. But on this one occasion, our differences collided for the goodness of our appetite (and yours!). A brief exchange regarding little beef sausages resulted in this moderately spiced dish. The smoked paprika definitely gives it that "oh my word" feel. The brief time in the pressure cooker condenses the ingredients into a strong flavor.

SERVES 6 TO 8

¼ cup (60 ml) olive oil (see tip)

1 yellow onion, sliced

4 cloves garlic, thinly sliced

½ tsp crushed red pepper flakes

½ red bell pepper, cut into ½"
(1.3-cm) julienne

1 tbsp (15 ml) white distilled vinegar

¼ tsp dried oregano

¼ tsp ground cumin

1 bay leaf

1 tsp (2.5 g) smoked paprika

1¼ tsp (7.5 g) kosher salt

6 oz (170 g) little beef sausages

½ cup (123 g) tomato sauce

1¼ cups (285 ml) water or Simple
Vegetable Broth (page 157)

1 large eggplant (about 8" [20-cm] long),
sliced into ½" (1.3-cm) rounds, halved
lengthwise on larger end

4 red potatoes, sliced into 1" (2.5-cm)
rounds, or 1 lb (455 g) fingerling potatoes

Heat the olive oil in the stovetop pressure cooker over medium or use the sauté function for the electric pressure cooker. Sauté the onion, garlic and red pepper flakes until the onion is translucent but not fully cooked, about 3 minutes. Add the bell pepper, vinegar, oregano, cumin, bay leaf, smoked paprika and salt. Stir and cook for 1 minute over medium heat for the stovetop cooker or maintain the sauté function for the electric cooker. Add the little beef sausages and tomato sauce. Stir and cook for an additional minute. Add the water or vegetable broth, eggplant and potatoes. Cancel cooking for the electric cooker. Season with salt and gently stir, covering the large vegetables. Close the lid.

Stovetop: Set to high pressure (15 PSI) and cook over high heat for 5 minutes total.

Electric: Set to high pressure (10–12 PSI) and 5 minutes.

When done, turn off the heat or turn off the cooker and allow the pressure to release on its own (natural-release). If pressure remains in the stovetop cooker after 10 minutes, transfer the cooker to the sink and apply the quick-release, or turn the valve to auto-release position for the electric. Open the cooker and adjust for salt.

Transfer the mélange to a deep casserole dish. Serve as a hearty stew or a main dish with Buttered Bacon Green Beans (page 170).

 B'S COOKING TIP: Avocado oil is pleasantly tasteful in this dish. If you have some, use it in lieu of the olive oil. Also, smoked chorizo is a tastier option if you like pork.

HEARTY SOUPS AND POTAJES

Slow cooking certain foods is a lovely way to appreciate the moment and really savor the permeated scents in your home. When you are short on time and need to feed a lot of hungry loved ones and want to stock up on robust and filling meals, the pressure cooker will save you a lot of valuable time. Soups, stews and chilis are some of the easiest foods you can prepare in the pressure cooker. It's basically one-pot cooking. Apart from the "Classic and Fusion Plates from My Cuban Kitchen" chapter, this one fills my heart with the most culinary lust. Every one of these recipes reinforces the ease of speed-cooking but also represents the love we share through memorable food. I suggest trying the Hearty Vegetable Soup (page 153) first. The Truffle and Tarragon Three-Bean Chili (page 154) will wow you too, though. It's the one chili I love making over and over again during cold months. It's fragrant, robust and elegant.

A note about these recipes—if working with an electric cooker, most of these are as simple as using the soup/stew function. In all cases, read through the recipe and check your cooker's manual if you have any technical questions.

My Dad's Ratatouille

I love this recipe for its simplicity and its very natural homage to the earth. All the ingredients in this traditional French stew come from the earth—ingredients workers spilled passion and hard work to harvest for our benefit. Those are the feelings this perfect-for-fall dish invoke. I fell in love with it only after my father mastered a combination that was perfect for our family. It's so good and so suited for effortless cooking, I don't see the need to wait 45 minutes to enjoy it. The magic of the pressure cooker will serve you a bowl of Provençal cuisine in just half the time, including prep. This is the epitome of one-stop, one-pot cooking. Add everything in at once and you're done! You know the drill with ratatouille: serve as the star dish, with rice, over pasta, or dip crusty French bread into it. Just enjoy it.

SERVES 6 TO 8

¼ cup (60 ml) plus 3 tbsp (45 ml) olive oil

1 medium red onion, chopped

1 medium Spanish onion, chopped

1 bulb garlic, peeled and thinly sliced

1 tsp (1 g) dried oregano

Leaves from 2 sprigs thyme

1 bay leaf

1 large eggplant, cut into 2" (5-cm) rounds and halved

1 green zucchini, cut into 1" (2.5-cm) slices

1 yellow summer squash, cut into 1" (2.5-cm) slices

1 red bell pepper, chopped

1 yellow bell pepper, chopped

6 Roma tomatoes, peeled and cut in half

1 cup (180 g) roasted tomatoes

¼ cup (60 ml) Simple Vegetable Broth (page 157), or store-bought

1 tbsp (18 g) kosher salt

Freshly ground black pepper

Fresh basil leaves, for garnish (optional)

Heat the 3 tablespoons (45 ml) of olive oil in the stovetop pressure cooker over medium, or use the sauté setting for the electric pressure cooker. Add all of the ingredients, except the basil, to the cooker in the order listed. Do not stir. Cancel cooking for the electric cooker, and close the lid.

Stovetop: Set to high pressure (15 PSI) and cook over high heat for 12 minutes total.

Electric: Set to high pressure (10–12 PSI) and 12–13 minutes.

When done, remove from the heat or turn off the cooker and release the pressure, using auto-release. Once all of the pressure is out, open the cooker, gently stir and adjust for salt. Transfer the stew to a deep casserole or Dutch oven for serving. Garnish with basil leaves or a few more thyme sprigs.

HEARTY VEGETABLE SOUP

When your time and energy are simply depleted, this is what I urge you to make. Not only will it take only ten minutes, the heartiness will make you feel better and replenish your soul. It's also a great soup to make for the people in your life needing some TLC.

SERVES 6

1 quart (946 ml) Herbed Chicken (page 166) or Beef Stock (page 167), or store-bought

2 cloves garlic, finely minced

1 tsp (6 g) kosher salt

1 medium onion, peeled and cut into 6 wedges

1 green bell pepper, quartered

1 green zucchini, sliced into 2" (2.5-cm) pieces

2 cups (180 g) roughly chopped cabbage

1 large carrot, sliced into 2" (2.5-cm) pieces

2 stalks celery, sliced into 1½" to 2" (2.5- to 5-cm) pieces

1 large beefsteak tomato, quartered, or 2 plum tomatoes

Kernels from 2 ears corn

Leaves from 2 sprigs rosemary

1 bunch curly parsley

½ tsp freshly ground white pepper

1 chayote squash, cut into 2" (5-cm) pieces

Add the stock, garlic and salt to the cooker. Bring to a boil over high heat for the stovetop pressure cooker, or use the sauté setting for the electric pressure cooker. Cook for about 4 minutes, then lower the heat to medium-low for the stovetop cooker or cancel cooking for the electric cooker, and add all the ingredients. Close the lid.

Stovetop: Set to high pressure (15 PSI) and cook over high heat for 10 minutes total.

Electric: Set to high pressure (10–12 PSI) and 8 minutes.

When done, remove the stovetop pressure cooker from the heat and apply quick-release, or turn off the electric pressure cooker and apply auto-release. When all of the pressure is out, open the cooker, adjust the salt and stir.

B'S COOKING TIP: All of the vegetables should be al dente, not hard or mushy, having maintained great vibrancy. If the vegetables are too hard, cook on high for 2 more minutes, then apply quick-release.

TRUFFLE AND TARRAGON THREE-BEAN CHILI

My love for delicate foods and strong flavors transcends cuisine. I love adding fragrant truffle oil to chili. It adds a silky texture to a really rustic American classic bowl of beans and meat. The sage also adds to its aroma. I used canned beans to save even more time.

SERVES 4 TO 6

1 tbsp (15 ml) canola oil

1½ lb (680 g) ground beef or ground turkey

1 tbsp (18 g) kosher salt

¼ tsp freshly ground black pepper

1 (16-oz [455-g]) can chickpeas, rinsed and drained

1 (16-oz [455-g]) can dark red kidney beans, rinsed and drained

1 (16-oz [455-g]) can black beans, rinsed and drained

5 Roma tomatoes, peeled and quartered

2½ cups (590 ml) unsalted Herbed Beef Stock (page 167), or store-bought

3 tbsp (45 ml) white truffle oil, plus more for drizzling

2 tbsp (28 ml) red wine vinegar

2½ tbsp (18 g) chili powder

¾ tsp ground cumin

1 tsp (1 g) dried oregano

1 tsp (6 g) black truffle salt

3 oz (85 g) tomato paste

1 bay leaf

5 leaves fresh tarragon, plus more for garnish

5 cloves garlic, finely minced

1 medium yellow onion, finely diced

Heat the canola oil in the stovetop pressure cooker over medium-high or use the sauté setting for the electric pressure cooker. Add the ground beef or turkey and break up, using a wooden fork. Season with the salt and cook over medium heat for the stovetop cooker or continue with the sauté setting for the electric cooker until the meat is lightly browned, 4 to 5 minutes. Add all of the ingredients to the cooker and stir to combine. Cancel cooking for the electric cooker, and close the lid.

Stovetop: Set to high pressure (15 PSI) and set the timer for 30 minutes. Cook over high heat until the pressure is reached, then lower the heat to medium and continue to cook.

Electric: Use the chili function, or set to high pressure (10–12 PSI) and 35 minutes.

When done, remove from the heat or turn off the cooker and allow the pressure to release on its own (natural-release). When all of the pressure is out, open the cooker and stir. Drizzle with a little more truffle oil and adjust for salt.

Serve over rice or as a large, hearty bowl. Top with minced tarragon and Havarti cheese, if desired.

SPICY TURKEY CHILI

I've been making this bold chili for my sister for a few years to much praise and seasonal request. I've not convinced her to enjoy the previous chili recipe, but I'll expect the spices in this one to entice her several times during fall and winter. It's spicy but not searing and the beans don't overpower the meat. It's really a great balance of proteins. This is truly ideal for the non-beef-eater who wants to enjoy a meaty chili. Of course, switch it out and use ground beef if you wish.

SERVES 6

2 tbsp (28 ml) olive oil

1 lb (455 g) ground turkey

½ cup (80 g) diced yellow onion

½ cup (80 g) diced red onion

½ cup (75 g) diced orange bell pepper

½ cup (75 g) diced red bell pepper

3 cloves garlic, minced

1 tbsp (3 g) dried oregano

4 tsp (10 g) chili powder

1 tbsp (15 ml) Worcestershire sauce

¼ tsp ground cumin

⅛ tsp ground cloves

1 tsp (5 g) dark brown sugar

2 cups (260 g) chunked Roma tomatoes

1 (16-oz [455-g]) can red kidney beans, drained and rinsed

2 tsp (12 g) kosher salt

1 cup (235 ml) Herbed Chicken Stock (page 166), or store-bought

Shredded cheddar cheese, for garnish (optional)

½ cup (24 g) sliced fresh chives, for garnish (optional)

½ cup (30 g) roughly chopped fresh cilantro, for garnish (optional)

Sour cream, for garnish (optional)

Heat the oil in the stovetop pressure cooker over medium-high or use the sauté setting for the electric pressure cooker. Add the turkey and brown, breaking up any chunks, about 3 to 6 minutes. For the stovetop cooker, lower the heat to medium; for the electric cooker, continue with the sauté setting. Add the vegetables. Stir and then continue adding the ingredients as listed, except the optional garnishes, making sure to keep stirring occasionally. Cancel cooking for the electric cooker, and close the lid.

Stovetop: Set to high pressure (15 PSI) and cook over high heat for 7 minutes.

Electric: Set to high pressure (10–12 PSI) and 10 minutes.

When done, remove from the heat or turn off the cooker and allow the pressure to release on its own (natural-release), about 5 to 7 minutes. If the pressure has not fully released after 7 minutes, apply auto-release. When all of the pressure is out, open the cooker and stir. Let simmer, uncovered, for 5 minutes while it thickens up.

Garnish individual servings with shredded cheddar cheese, chives, cilantro, sour cream or all.

 B'S COOKING TIP: I consider the heat level in this chili to be medium. It's too spicy for my palate, so I enjoy it with 1 less teaspoon (3 g) of chili powder. To add a bit more of a kick, add 1 more teaspoon (3 g) of chili powder or ½ teaspoon of seeded jalapeño.

SIMPLE VEGETABLE BROTH

The beauty of making stocks and broths in the pressure cooker is the flexibility of different batch sizes. You can make smaller batches in fifteen minutes for same-day use. It could take you the same amount of time to run to the market for a carton of broth not as amazing as your own creation. Once you get the hang of pressure cooking, play around with your broth ingredients. A lot of the recipes in this book use this veggie broth.

YIELDS 2 QUARTS (1.9 L) BROTH

¼ cup (60 ml) olive oil

4 large heirloom tomatoes, quartered

2 chayote squash, quartered

1 bulb garlic, skin on, halved crosswise

1 lb (455 g) celery, with leaves

5 medium carrots, cut into big pieces

1 green bell pepper, halved

1 red bell pepper, halved

1 large Spanish onion, skin on, quartered

1 bunch fresh cilantro or parsley

2 bay leaves

Salt and freshly ground black pepper

1½ quarts (1.4 L) water

Heat the oil in the stovetop pressure cooker over medium or use the sauté setting for the electric pressure cooker. Add all of the ingredients, except the water. Brown the vegetables, stirring occasionally, about 4 minutes. Pour the water over the vegetables. Cancel cooking for the electric cooker, and close the lid.

Stovetop: Set to high pressure (15 PSI) and set the timer for 35 minutes. Cook over high heat until the pressure point is reached, then lower the heat to medium and continue to cook.

Electric: Set to high pressure (10–12 PSI) and 35 minutes.

When done, remove from the heat or turn off the cooker and allow the pressure to release on its own (natural-release), about 10 minutes. If there's pressure in the cooker at 10 minutes, turn the valve to auto-release to finish letting the pressure out. When it is all out, open the cooker and stir. Adjust the salt and pepper. Strain the broth through a sieve or large colander into a large bowl. Discard the cooked vegetables. Transfer the broth to glass or plastic storage containers, uncovered. Allow it to cool before covering and chilling.

B'S COOKING TIP: Freeze the broth and it will keep for up to 3 months. When ready to use, thaw in the refrigerator for a few hours before using.

For a darker broth, add 12 ounces (340 g) of clean, whole cremini mushrooms.

Hearty Vegetable Stock Purée

Add a bit of girth to your stocks and broths by adding an additional amount of parcooked vegetables. You can even do this to store-purchased stock, and instantly, you have a wonderful purée that will round out many dishes.

YIELDS 2½ QUARTS (2.4 L) STOCK PURÉE

3 cups (710 ml) Simple Vegetable Broth (page 157), or store-bought

6 stalks celery, with leaves

4 medium carrots, cut into 1½" (4-cm) pieces

2 tomatoes on the vine, halved

1 green bell pepper, chopped

1 chayote squash, peeled and cubed

1 yellow onion, quartered

6 cloves garlic

1 bunch parsley, chopped

Salt and freshly ground black pepper

Add all of the ingredients to the pressure cooker. Stir and close the lid.

Stovetop: Set to low pressure (8 PSI) and cook over medium-high heat for 5 minutes total.

Electric: Set to high pressure (10–12 PSI) and 7 minutes.

When done, remove the stovetop pressure cooker from the heat and do a quick-release, or turn off the electric pressure cooker and apply auto-release. When the pressure is out, open the lid and transfer the entire contents of the cooker to a high-power food processor. In batches, process on high speed for 30 to 60 seconds, or until the carrots and celery are fully broken down. Transfer back to the cooker and adjust for salt. Transfer to storage containers.

B'S COOKING NOTE: The vegetables should not be fully cooked after cooking in the pressure cooker. The cooking time is simply to soften them enough to process. Depending on the size and power of your food processor, you may have to do this in 2 to 4 steps.

Conscious Living and Eating

While I was growing up, my parents were extremely stern when it came to not wasting food. At the time, I didn't understand their demand we eat everything on the plate. I get it now. I am very adamant about not being wasteful and I make conscious decisions in the kitchen to use everything. Very little goes to waste when I cook. A rustic version of this purée is a reflection of that philosophy. Remnants of your vegetable stock or broth with these raw vegetables turn into a dense purée that adds depth to just about anything. For a thinner, more flavorful purée, add 1 cup (225 g) of the reserved cooked vegetables from the original vegetable stock recipe and pulse until well blended. This will add more depth and tremendous flavor to soups, chilis and so on.

FULLY STOCKED PHO

Another benefit of the pressure cooker is exploring other cuisines! Vietnamese pho is so far removed from my forté and cultural knowledge, but I've been impressed with every bowl I've tasted. They were all so simple but so tasty. The stocks have subtle notes of acid, sweetness and smoke. The meats vary in texture and fat, offering a finish unlike many other soups I like. My affection for pho led to a craft session in my kitchen that lasted about one month. I did a lot of market research (a.k.a. taste testing in three cities) before settling on this fully stocked pho. The combination of oxtail, tongue and sirloin upgrades a simple stock to a memorable herbal bowl.

SERVES 4

8 oz (225 g) dried rice noodles

3 whole cloves

1 tsp (2 g) fennel seeds

3 bay leaves

2 tbsp (12 g) peeled and minced fresh ginger

2 whole star anise

2½ quarts (2.4 L) water

1 lb (455 g) oxtail

3 oz (85 g) beef tongue, thinly sliced

1 medium onion, unpeeled, quartered

5 cloves garlic, minced

¼ cup (60 ml) Asian fish sauce

2 tsp (12 g) kosher salt

¼ lb (115 g) sirloin, thinly sliced

11 oz (310 g) bean sprouts

½ jalapeño pepper, sliced

3 spring onions per serving, sliced

1 to 2 large bunches fresh Thai basil, for garnish

Sriracha sauce (optional)

Hoisin sauce (optional)

Place the noodles in a large Dutch oven or pot and cover with room-temperature water for 1 hour, allowing them to soften. Place the cloves, fennel seeds, bay leaves, ginger and star anise in a cloth tea bag (mousseline) and tie. Add the water, oxtail, beef tongue, onion, garlic, fish sauce and spice pouch to the cooker, then season with salt. Stir and close the lid.

Stovetop: Set to high pressure (15 PSI) and cook over high for 30 minutes total.

Electric: Set to high pressure (10–12 PSI) and 30 minutes.

When done, remove from the heat or cancel cooking and allow the pressure to release on its own (natural-release), about 20 minutes. Open the cooker and remove the oxtail and beef tongue, using tongs. Set aside. Strain the liquid through a colander, reserving all of the stock. Discard the spice pouch and onion, including the peel.

Transfer the liquid back to the cooker. Add the rice noodles. Cook for 3 minutes, uncovered, over high heat for the stovetop pressure cooker or using the sauté setting for the electric pressure cooker. Strain again, reserving all of the liquid. When done, remove from the heat or cancel cooking.

Ladle 1½ to 2 cups (355 to 475 ml) of the broth into each serving bowl. Evenly distribute the noodles, oxtail, beef tongue and sirloin among each serving. Allow it to rest for 2 minutes until the sirloin looks like it's starting to brown. To each bowl, add desired amount of bean sprouts, jalapeño and spring onions. Garnish with basil sprigs. If desired, stir in hot sauce and hoisin sauce.

Not Your Average Chicken Soup

I've learned over the years there's truth to the title "Chicken Soup for the Soul." My mother's chicken soup has healed some really ill friends. It's a very real phenomenon. I still ask her to make some when I'm sick. Enjoy the time savings in this special soup, especially when nursing your loved ones back to health.

SERVES 4 TO 6

6 tbsp (90 ml) canola oil

2 yellow onions, 1 chopped and 1 quartered

7 cloves garlic, minced

1 bay leaf

1 chicken, cut into parts (cut breasts into 1" [2.5-cm] pieces, leaving all other parts whole)

⅛ tsp ground cumin

1 tbsp (18 g) salt

¼ tsp freshly ground black pepper

5 cups (1.2 L) water

3 ears corn, cut in thirds

1 red bell pepper, seeded and cut into 1" (2.5-cm) pieces

3 stalks celery, chopped

2 carrots, chopped

1 bunch cilantro

Juice of 2 limes, for serving

Add the canola oil, chopped onion, garlic and bay leaf to the cooker. Cook over medium heat for the stovetop pressure cooker or use the sauté setting for the electric pressure cooker, until the onion is translucent and garlic is fragrant, about 5 minutes. Add the chicken and season with cumin, salt and pepper. Brown on both sides, gently stirring and making sure the chicken does not stick, about 4 minutes. Add all of the remaining ingredients, except the cilantro and lime juice. Cancel cooking for the electric cooker, and close the lid.

Stovetop: Set to high pressure (15 PSI) and set the timer for 11 minutes. Cook over high heat until the pressure point has been reached, then lower the heat to medium or high enough to maintain the high pressure point.

Electric: Set to high pressure (10–12 PSI) and 10–11 minutes.

When done, remove from the heat or turn off the cooker and release the pressure, using auto-release. When all of the pressure is out, open the cooker and adjust for salt and pepper. Garnish each serving with fresh cilantro and a hand squeeze of fresh lime.

B'S COOKING TIP: You may leave the chicken breasts in 1-inch (2.5-cm) pieces. Alternatively you may pull the breast, lengthwise, into 2-inch (5-cm) strips.

B CREATIVE! During the fall and winter months, add 2 cups (280 g) of seeded and cubed acorn squash, or your preferred winter squash, keeping cooking times in mind. During the summer, top individual servings with slices of Haas avocados. There are no true rules. So, simply add both if and when you want and love it the same.

Pumpkin Coconut Curry Soup

I fell in love with the open-air farmers' market in Fiji. Two floors of aisles were lined with burlap bags filled to the brim with spices, some of which I was unfamiliar with. Seeing women slowly peruse each vendor as they chose their week's bounty inspired me to get to know spices in a more intimate way. I could see the love that they had stored up for their family meals. I left with bags full of a variety of herbs and spices, including the curry I used to make all of the dishes in this book. I share this soup because I've loved a myriad of versions since I could remember. It embodies a warmth and subtle richness, rendering it perfect for cold nights. The touch of toasted coconut and pumpkin seeds beautifully completes it.

SERVES 4 TO 6

1 tbsp (15 ml) peanut oil

1 yellow onion, chopped

4 cloves garlic, minced

½ tsp ground cloves

⅛ tsp ground cumin

2 tsp (4 g) curry powder

2 cups (475 ml) Herbed Chicken Stock (page 166), or store-bought

2 cups (475 ml) coconut milk

2½ cups (368 g) pumpkin purée

2 tbsp (28 ml) liquid sugar

1 tbsp (6 g) minced fresh ginger

4 mint leaves, rubbed and chopped

1 tsp (12 g) kosher salt

¼ cup (20 g) toasted shaved coconut, for garnish

¼ cup (35 g) toasted pumpkin seeds, for garnish

Heat the peanut oil in the stovetop pressure cooker over medium-high or use the sauté setting for the electric pressure cooker. Add the onion and garlic and sauté until the onion begins to soften and the garlic is fragrant but not browned, about 2 minutes. Using a wooden spoon, stir in the cloves, cumin and curry powder. Add the chicken broth and coconut milk and bring to a boil, uncovered. Lower the heat to a simmer for the stovetop cooker or cancel cooking for the electric cooker, and stir in the pumpkin purée and liquid sugar. Add the ginger and mint leaves. Season with the salt and close the lid.

Stovetop: Set to high pressure (15 PSI) and cook over high heat for 8 minutes total.

Electric: Set to high pressure (10–12 PSI) and 8 minutes.

When done, remove from the heat or turn off the cooker and allow the pressure to release on its own (natural-release), about 3 to 5 minutes. When all of the pressure is out, open the cooker and allow the soup to sit for about 5 minutes. Place an immersion blender into the cooker and blend on medium speed, maintaining a circular motion, until the soup is smooth, about 2 minutes. If you don't have an immersion blender, transfer the soup to a high-powered food processor and blend on high speed until the soup is smooth with no signs of the vegetables. Blend in batches if necessary. Transfer back to the pressure cooker or your serving dish. Stir and adjust for salt.

Garnish individual servings with toasted coconut shavings and pumpkin seeds.

CARROT, GINGER AND TARRAGON SOUP

I first had carrot soup in 1999 while dining at a boutique restaurant in the Woodley Park neighborhood of Washington, D.C. I fell in love then and think about it still. This is inspired, in part, by those memories of sinking into my seat in my favorite city and savoring fresh carrots and spicy ginger puréed into a really colorful and smooth soup. The tarragon serves as a beautiful top layer of fragrance. The short cooking time for a nice-size batch keeps it on rotation during fall and winter.

SERVES 4 TO 6

2 tbsp (28 g) uncultured salted butter

1 lb (455 g) carrots, sliced

1 tbsp (6 g) minced fresh ginger

1 medium onion, diced

1 shallot, sliced

Leaves from 2 sprigs tarragon, plus more for garnish, or 2 tsp (1 g) dried

1½ cups (355 ml) unsalted chicken broth

1½ cups (355 ml) orange juice

2 tsp (12 g) salt

½ tsp freshly grated nutmeg, plus more for finishing

3 tbsp (45 ml) Grand Marnier or other good-quality orange liqueur

3 tbsp (45 ml) honey or agave nectar

¼ tsp freshly ground white pepper

Melt the butter in the stovetop pressure cooker over medium heat, or use the sauté setting for the electric pressure cooker. Add the carrots, ginger, onion, shallot and tarragon and cook until the onion begins to soften, about 3 minutes. Add the chicken broth and bring to a boil. Reduce the heat to low for the stovetop cooker or cancel cooking for the electric cooker, and add the orange juice. Season with the salt, add the nutmeg and close the lid.

Stovetop: Set to high pressure (15 PSI) and cook over high heat for 10 minutes total.

Electric: Set to high pressure (10–12 PSI) and 12 minutes.

When done, turn off the heat or turn off the cooker and allow the pressure to release on its own (natural-release), about 5 minutes. When all of the pressure is out, open the cooker and let sit for 5 minutes. Place an immersion blender into the cooker and blend on medium speed, maintaining a circular motion, until the soup is smooth, about 1 minute. If you don't have an immersion blender, transfer the soup to a high-powered food processor or blender and blend on high speed until all of the ingredients are well-blended and smooth. Blend in batches if necessary. Transfer the soup back to the cooker. Stir in the Grand Marnier, honey and white pepper. Adjust for salt. Simmer for 5 minutes, uncovered. Garnish with fresh tarragon sprigs, and adjust with more nutmeg, if desired.

CREAMY ROASTED TOMATO BISQUE

This soup is incredibly simple and full of earthiness and aroma. Using tomatoes in season are best, but you can still enjoy most varieties during the off-season with the subtle acidity balanced with celery and Parmesan. Entice your guests at your next dinner soirée by serving this as a shooter in pretty shot glasses or demitasses.

SERVES 4 TO 6

5 Roma tomatoes, halved

3 large tomatoes, quartered (heirlooms are a great option)

7 cloves garlic, mashed

⅓ cup (80 ml) olive oil

2 tsp (12 g) kosher salt

2 tsp (2 g) dried oregano

1 large Spanish onion, chopped

1 stalk celery, chopped

2 tbsp (32 g) tomato paste

½ bunch flat-leaf parsley

3 cups (475 ml) Herbed Chicken Stock (page 166), or store-bought

1 cup (235 ml) heavy whipping cream

Leaves from 3 sprigs thyme

½ tsp freshly ground black pepper

Grated Parmesan cheese, for garnish

3 sprigs thyme, for garnish

Preheat the oven to 425°F (220°C). In a large bowl, combine the tomatoes, garlic and olive oil, and season with the salt and oregano. Mix well. Transfer to large baking sheet or oven-safe deep casserole dish and spread out evenly. Place the baking sheet in the middle of the rack and roast for 30 minutes.

Carefully remove from the oven and transfer the tomatoes to the cooker. Add all of the remaining ingredients, except the Parmesan and 3 whole thyme sprigs. Gently stir the contents inside the cooker, using a large wooden spoon. Close the lid.

Stovetop: Set to high pressure (15 PSI) and cook over high heat for 10 minutes total.

Electric: Use the soup/stew setting, or set to high pressure (10–12 PSI) and 10 minutes.

When done, remove from the heat or turn off the cooker and release the pressure, using auto-release. When all of the pressure is out, open the cooker and let sit for 5 minutes. Place an immersion blender into the cooker and blend on medium speed, maintaining a circular motion, until the soup is smooth, about 1 minute. If you don't have an immersion blender, transfer the soup to a high-powered food processor and blend on high speed until all of the ingredients are broken down and well blended, about 1 to 2 minutes. You want to achieve a very smooth texture. Blend in batches if necessary. Transfer the soup back to the cooker and stir. Adjust for salt.

Garnish each serving with grated Parmesan and the remaining thyme. Serve with crusty bread.

WILD MUSHROOM VELOUTÉ

I grew up eating canned cream of mushroom soup and I remember begging my mother for more every time we had it. God knows I'd never do that now, nor would I ever suggest anyone use it unless dire and unique circumstances (or recipes) call for it. I do pardon my mother since she was steadily feeding a family of seven and her intention was honest. Plus, it resulted in a true appreciation for a velvety, *en blanc* soup. I enjoy making this soup more than I can articulate. It's the consummate combination of earthy, silky and savory. This is a perfect example of the *Joy of Cooking* really coming to life.

SERVES 4 TO 6

Mushroom Stock

8 oz (225 g) baby bella mushrooms, stemmed and sliced

4 oz (115 g) white-cap mushrooms, stemmed and sliced

4 oz (115 g) cremini mushrooms, stemmed and sliced

4 tbsp (55 g) unsalted butter

1 yellow onion, small-diced

3 cloves garlic, mashed

1 sprig thyme

1 bay leaf

4¼ cups (1 L) water

Soup

3 tbsp (41 g) unsalted butter

2 whole leeks, cut crosswise demilune *and minced*

Leaves from 1 sprig thyme

1 tsp (6 g) kosher salt

⅛ tsp freshly ground white pepper

¼ cup (30 g) all-purpose flour

½ cup (120 ml) dry white cooking wine

½ cup (120 ml) sherry

1½ cups (355 ml) heavy whipping cream

Clean the mushrooms with a paper towel and reserve the sliced mushrooms for the soup. Then, prepare the mushroom stock: Melt the 4 tablespoons (55 g) of butter in the pressure cooker over medium-high heat for the stovetop pressure cooker or use the sauté setting for the electric pressure cooker. Sauté the onion and garlic until fragrant, about 2 minutes. Add the thyme sprig and the bay leaf, mushroom stems and water. Stir, cancel cooking for the electric cooker and close the lid.

Stovetop: Set to high pressure (15 PSI) and cook over high heat for 6 minutes total.

Electric: Set to high pressure (10–12 PSI) and 6 minutes.

When done, remove the stovetop cooker from the heat and transfer to the sink and release the pressure using quick-release, or cancel cooking for the electric cooker and apply auto-release. When all of the pressure is out, open the cooker and strain the broth, reserving the mushroom mixture for later use (such as in the Cheesy Broccoli Mushroom Casserole on page 179).

Prepare the soup: In the same cooker, melt the butter over medium heat for the stovetop pressure cooker or use the sauté setting for the electric pressure cooker. Cook the leeks and thyme leaves until they begin to brown, about 3 to 4 minutes. Stir in the sliced mushrooms and cook for 3 to 4 minutes. Season with the salt and pepper. Whisk in the flour, stirring constantly, for about 30 seconds, making sure to avoid clumping. Stir in the mushroom broth, white cooking wine and sherry. Cancel cooking for the electric cooker, and close the lid.

Stovetop: Set to high pressure (15 PSI) and cook over high heat for 10 minutes total.

Electric: Set to high pressure (10–12 PSI) and 10 minutes.

When done, remove from the heat or turn off the cooker and release the pressure, using auto-release. When all of the pressure is out, open the cooker and stir in the cream. Adjust for salt and pepper. Garnish each individual serving with additional thyme, if desired. Serve immediately.

*See photo on page 148.

Herbed Chicken Stock

Due to the lack of decent food and resources in Cuba, and presumably many poor parts of the world, it is commonplace, mostly out of sheer necessity, to use water instead of a flavorful bone stock in liquid-based foods. However, as much meat as Americans and people in other developed countries have access to and consume, chicken stock should be something we do by default instead of using basic water. This recipe will convince you it's worth the easy effort. After time, you can modify and tweak the seasonings to your liking. This will get you started and keep you excited about boasting a true "scratch-made" recipe.

Yields 2¾ quarts (2.6 L) stock

3 lb (1.4 kg) chicken neck and back bones

6 stalks celery with leaves, cut in half

5 carrots, cut in half

2 Spanish onions, 1 with skin on, quartered

1 bulb garlic, skin on, halved

2 tbsp (36 g) kosher salt

1 tsp (2 g) freshly ground black pepper

3 spring onions

1 green bell pepper, quartered

2 bay leaves

12 sprigs thyme

12 sprigs parsley

3¼ quarts (3 L) cold water

Add all of the ingredients to the pressure cooker, stir and close the lid.

Stovetop: Set to high pressure (15 PSI) and set the timer for 50 minutes. Cook over high heat until the pressure has been reached, about 24 minutes, then lower the heat to medium and continue to cook.

Electric: Set to high pressure (10–12 PSI) and 60 minutes.

When done, remove from the heat or turn off the cooker and allow the pressure to release on its own (natural-release), about 15 minutes. When all of the pressure is out, open the cooker and strain the stock, using a sturdy colander, retaining only the liquid. Reserve the vegetables for the Hearty Vegetable Stock Purée recipe on page 158. Transfer the liquid to a large pot and allow to cool before covering. Chill the stock overnight. Skim off the top layer of fat and then transfer the stock to glass storage containers. Maintain refrigerated until ready to use. Enjoy this!

 B'S COOKING TIP: Freeze the stock and it will keep for up to 3 months. Allow to thaw in the refrigerator before using.

Herbed Beef Stock

This is the beefy version of the Herbed Chicken Stock (page 166), only it has more color and a few complementing ingredients. Like the Simple Vegetable Broth (page 157) and the chicken stock, I also use this a lot throughout this book.

Yields 2¾ quarts (2.6 L) stock

3 lb (1.4 kg) beef bones, cut into 2" (5-cm) pieces

6 stalks celery with leaves, cut in half

5 carrots, cut in half

2 Spanish onions, skin on, quartered

1 bulb garlic, halved, skin on

12 oz (340 g) whole mushrooms

1 oz (28 g) tomato paste

2 tbsp (36 g) kosher salt

1 tsp (2 g) freshly ground black pepper, or 10 whole peppercorns

3 spring onions

3 bay leaves

12 sprigs thyme

12 sprigs parsley

3¼ quarts (3 L) cold water

½ cup (120 ml) red wine (optional)

Add all of the ingredients to the pressure cooker, stir and close the lid.

Stovetop: Set to high pressure (15 PSI) and set the timer for 60 minutes. Cook over high heat until the pressure has been reached, about 26 minutes, then lower the heat to medium and continue to cook for the remaining 34 minutes.

Electric: Set to high pressure (10–12 PSI) and 60 minutes.

When done, remove from the heat or turn off the cooker and allow the pressure to release on its own (natural-release), about 17 minutes. When all of the pressure is out, open the cooker and strain the stock, using a sturdy colander, retaining only the liquid. You may reserve the vegetables for the Hearty Vegetable Stock Purée recipe on page 158. Transfer the liquid to a large pot and allow to cool before covering. Chill overnight. Skim the top layer of fat and then transfer the stock to glass storage containers. Maintain refrigerated until ready to use.

B'S COOKING TIPS: Ask your local butcher to saw off for you your desired amount of beef bones for stocks and other purposes. That will be much easier than buying a prepacked package, especially since you can ask for a specific amount. They'll do this for all of your other fresh meats, too.

Freeze the stock and it will keep for up to 3 months. Allow to thaw in the refrigerator before using.

GREENS AND VEGETABLES

You may wonder, "Why pressure-cook greens and vegetables?" One of the joys of cooking under pressure is the tremendous amount of flavor you preserve by lessening your cooking time by up to 70 percent. Your mashed potatoes will retain all of their iron, your cauliflower will fill you with plenty of calcium, and your broccoli will remain close to its raw brightness. Plus, your vegetables won't be so hollow and limp from spending so much time in water! I invite you to try the Vibrant Beet Mashed Potatoes (page 175). Their color is seductive. I'm particularly proud of that dish because it convinced me red beets are a beautiful vegetable to work with regardless of their stain. Until now, I've not given them the love they deserve, mostly eating them roasted in specific salads. I love pairing those whipped potatoes with Your New Favorite Beef Tongue Dish (page 51) in the second chapter. You will also enjoy making smoky collard greens in just 30 minutes. They will never take up three hours of your time again. Ever.

Buttered Bacon Green Beans

This is a Thanksgiving favorite at home. Their fast cook time helps reduce the stress associated with so much cooking during the holidays. Another way I enjoy them is with a drizzle of white truffle oil. The bacon takes simple green beans to another level of flavor for anyone looking for something more than vegetables.

Serves 4 to 6

10 oz (280 g) Black Forest uncured bacon, cut into small cubes

12 tbsp (1½ sticks [167 g]) cultured butter, divided

½ bulb or 12 cloves garlic, sliced

2 lb (905 g) fresh green beans, ends trimmed

1 tsp (6 g) onion salt

⅛ tsp freshly ground white pepper

½ cup (120 ml) Herbed Chicken Stock (page 166), or store-bought

Heat the stovetop pressure cooker over high heat, or use the sauté setting for the electric pressure cooker. Add the bacon and cook for 4 minutes, stirring a few times. Add 8 tablespoons (1 stick [112 g]) of the butter and the garlic. Sauté the garlic until fragrant but not browned, about 2 minutes. Add the remaining 4 tablespoons (55 g) of butter and melt. In batches, work in the beans, smothering them fully until they're all covered with the garlic butter. Season with the onion salt and white pepper. Top off with the chicken stock. Stir, cancel cooking for the electric cooker and close the lid.

Stovetop: Set to high pressure (15 PSI) and cook over high heat for 6 minutes total.

Electric: Set to high pressure (10–12 PSI) and 8 minutes.

When done, remove the stovetop cooker from the heat and transfer to the sink and release the pressure, using quick-release, or turn off the electric cooker and apply auto-release. When all of the pressure is out, open the cooker and strain, reserving the extra butter liquid. Transfer the beans to a serving platter. Ladle the garlic butter sauce over the beans. The sauce is also really nice over mashed potatoes or any other roasted vegetable dish you make.

B CREATIVE! Love mushrooms? For an earthier and even "meatier" bowl of green beans, lightly sear 8 ounces (227 g) of your favorite mushrooms when you add the bacon. If you do this, reduce the stock to ¼ cup (60 ml). I also enjoy this dish with caramelized onions; simply slice and add with the mushrooms. The possibilities are endless!

RUSTIC GARLICKY MASHED POTATOES

Peru is known for having centuries-old varieties of potatoes, somewhere along the lines of over 100. Needless to say, Peruvians are really creative when it comes to working with potatoes. I particularly enjoy one of the bold yellow varieties. In far contrast, I learned how to appreciate a very refined technique of whipping potatoes into a very delicate *quenelle* from world-famous chef Joël Robuchon. His are really white, really fluffy and really fancy. Those two experiences have changed my approach to making and whipping potatoes at home. For everyday enjoyment and when needing a starchy side, these potatoes are it. The aroma reminds me of a chilly fall day in Val de Loire, France, where I spent some time in 2006 when casually studying the Provençal region.

SERVES 4

5 large brown or russet potatoes, washed and quartered

1½ cups (355 ml) water

1 cup (235 ml) heavy whipping cream

½ cup (120 ml) whole or 2% milk

1½ tsp (9 g) kosher or pink Himalayan salt

2 sprigs rosemary

5 large cloves garlic, pressed

4 tbsp (55 g) unsalted butter

Add all of the ingredients except the butter to the pressure cooker, but do not stir. Close the lid.

Stovetop: Set to high pressure (15 PSI) and cook over high heat for 15 minutes total.

Electric: Set to high pressure (10–12 PSI) and 15 minutes.

When done, turn off the heat or turn off the cooker and allow the pressure to release on its own (natural-release), about 7 to 10 minutes. When all of the pressure is out, open the cooker and remove the rosemary sprigs. Add the butter, and mash the potatoes, using a potato masher, until your mash is creamy and most of the potatoes are completely broken down. It's okay to have a few chunky pieces throughout. Adjust for salt.

 B'S COOKING TIP: Do not press the garlic so hard that you have a really fine paste. Simply press enough to scrape big, flat pieces. And for even smoother results, peel the potatoes completely.

Cheesy Cauliflower Purée

Cauliflower is quickly gaining some deserved popularity in American cuisine. It's a much healthier and lighter option to mashed potatoes and is flexible enough to incorporate into your diet. Boiling or steaming it conventionally would drain an already low-profile vegetable. In the pressure cooker, you're sure to retain every bit of its nutrients and natural earthiness. The smoked Gouda does the trick and elevates its impact. This is incredibly nice with blackened salmon or the Old-School, New-School Poached Cuban-Style Meat Loaf on page 67.

Serves 4 to 6

2 heads cauliflower

2 tbsp (28 g) unsalted butter

2 tsp (10 ml) extra-virgin olive oil

3 cloves garlic, minced

1½ cups (355 ml) water

1 tsp (6 g) kosher salt, plus more to taste

1 cup (120 g) shredded smoked Gouda cheese

½ cup (120 ml) heavy whipping cream

Freshly ground white pepper

Spring onions, chopped, for garnish (optional)

Cut the stalk off the cauliflower. Rinse and pat dry. Place on a baking sheet or cutting board. Rub the cauliflower with butter, covering it well. Separate the florets from the heads. Heat the olive oil in the stovetop pressure cooker over medium-low or use the simmer setting for the electric pressure cooker. Sauté the garlic until lightly browned, about 30 seconds. Do not allow the garlic to burn. Lower the heat immediately for the stovetop cooker or cancel cooking for the electric cooker. Add the florets to the cooker and stir once. Add the water and season with the salt. Close the lid.

Stovetop: Set to high pressure (15 PSI) and cook over high heat for 13 minutes total.

Electric: Set to high pressure (10–12 PSI) and 13 minutes.

When done, remove from the heat or cancel cooking and allow the pressure to release on its own (natural-release), about 6 minutes. When all of the pressure is out, open the cooker and drain the cauliflower. Mash the cauliflower, using a potato masher, until mostly smooth, and return it to the cooker.

Return the stovetop pressure cooker to the stove over low heat or set the electric pressure cooker to the simmer setting. Fold in the cheese until melted and well blended. Whisk in the cream and stir until you have a smooth and creamy purée. Season with pepper and adjust for salt. Garnish with spring onions, if desired.

 B'S COOKING TIP: For some added crunch, aroma and texture, top with shaved fennel, using a vegetable peeler.

VIBRANT BEET MASHED POTATOES

Did you ever think potatoes could be so sexy? This creative combination came to mind while shopping at my local farmers' market, where the potatoes and beets were propped next to each other. An idea just clicked. Adding a less popular vegetable to a staple side is a great way to introduce it to many other dishes. The toughness of each is quickly softened in the cooker for unexpected brightness. The beets add a noticeable amount of delicate sweetness and the potatoes keep the mash creamy. Enjoy this with the Tarragon-Mustard Braised Short Ribs on page 56; the pairing is delectable.

SERVES 4 TO 6

3 small to medium beets, peeled and cut in half

5 large white potatoes, peeled and cut in half

1 cup (235 ml) water

1 tsp (6 g) kosher salt

1 cup (235 ml) heavy whipping cream

3 tbsp (42 g) butter

1 bunch cilantro, chopped

¼ tsp freshly ground white pepper

1 spring onion, chopped diagonally

Submerge the beets in a bowl of water, enough to cover them, for 15 minutes or until the water is bright red. Reserve 1 cup (235 ml) of this water. Add the potatoes, beets, water and the reserved beet juice water to the pressure cooker. Season with the salt. Stir and close the lid.

Stovetop: Set to high pressure (15 PSI) and cook over high heat for 13 minutes total.

Electric: Set to high pressure (10–12 PSI) and 18 minutes.

When done, remove from the heat or turn off the cooker and allow the pressure to release on its own (natural-release), about 7 to 8 minutes. If the pressure has not fully released after 8 minutes, apply auto-release. When all of the pressure is out, open the cooker and mash the vegetables, using a potato masher, until chunky but rustic. Whip in the cream and butter until creamy. Fold in cilantro and season with the white pepper.

Garnish with spring onion. For creamier potatoes, add an additional ½ cup (120 ml) of cream and 1 tablespoon (14 g) of butter.

SOUTHERN-STYLE STEWED TOMATOES

Michie Tavern in Charlottesville, Virginia, has the best stewed tomatoes I've ever eaten. I used to frequent that historical cabin restaurant simply to enjoy those luscious and juicy tomatoes. The experience was all the rave, and guests are entertained by men and women servers dressed in period costumes.

This dish is a great weekend breakfast option. Traditionally, this was served with fried chicken and collard greens, but an updated approach would be to pour them over polenta, couscous or to include them as one-third of a vegetable triad. A juicy steak pairing would be delightful. This is my instant interpretation.

SERVES 4 TO 6

3 tbsp (42 g) salted cultured butter

5 tbsp (75 g) light brown sugar

Leaves from 2 sprigs rosemary

1 bay leaf

1 cup (160 g) diced yellow onion

4 beefsteak tomatoes, quartered

3 (16-oz [455-g]) cans tomatoes

½ cup (120 ml) water or Simple Vegetable Broth (page 157)

1½ tsp (9 g) kosher salt

3 sweet biscuits or butter flake rolls

Hard cow's milk cheese, for garnish (optional)

Melt the butter in the stovetop pressure cooker over medium-high heat or use the simmer setting for the electric pressure cooker. Stir in the brown sugar, rosemary, bay leaf and onion and cook for 1 minute. Add the tomatoes and water or vegetable broth. Season with the salt and stir. Add the biscuits and mix well to blend the ingredients. Cancel cooking for the electric cooker, and close the lid.

Stovetop: Set to high pressure (15 PSI) and cook over high heat for 3 minutes total.

Electric: Set to high pressure (10–12 PSI) and 5 minutes.

When done, remove from the heat or turn off the cooker and allow the pressure to release on its own (natural-release), about 4 minutes. When all of the pressure is out, open the cooker and remove the bay leaf. Adjust for salt. Stir well to combine the biscuits and tomatoes. If whole biscuits remain, gently break them apart to blend in well with the tomatoes. Serve warm or cold. Grate the cheese over the top, if desired.

 B'S COOKING TIP: The biscuits make a noticeable difference. Use your favorite flaky biscuits but do keep in mind how they contribute to the dish. Day-old corn bread is a great alternative I enjoy from time to time.

CARIBBEAN CURRIED CABBAGE AND VEGETABLES

I remember a cold salad my mother used to make when we lived in Miami, shortly after leaving Cuba. It was creamy with shredded carrots and raisins. Food has a way of staying with you. That salad doesn't even resemble this recipe, but it inspired me to make these vibrant vegetables with added spices, widening its appeal. Serve as a side vegetable dish; it pairs nicely with stewed lamb or the Old-School, New-School Poached Cuban-Style Meat Loaf on page 67. Alternatively, serve over hot jasmine rice.

SERVES 4 TO 6

1 tbsp (14 g) coconut spread or butter

4 cloves garlic, minced

1 red onion, sliced

1 leek, chopped into 2" (5-cm) pieces

1 tbsp (6 g) curry powder

1 tsp (2 g) cayenne pepper

½ tsp ground allspice

3 cups (360 g) rainbow carrots, cut diagonally into 1" (2.5-cm) pieces

½ red bell pepper, cut into ½" (5-cm) julienne

1 napa cabbage, roughly chopped

1 cup (145 g) raisins or dates

1 cup (235 ml) water or Simple Vegetable Broth (page 157)

2 tsp (12 g) kosher salt

Freshly ground white pepper

Heat the coconut spread in the stovetop pressure cooker over medium-high or use the sauté setting for the electric pressure cooker. Sauté the garlic, onion and leek for 1 minute. Add the curry powder, cayenne and allspice, stirring until the vegetables are well-coated, about 2 minutes. Stir in the carrots and bell pepper, coating them as well. Reduce the heat to low for the stovetop cooker or cancel the sauté setting for the electric cooker and use the residual heat to continue cooking while you add the rest of the ingredients. Add the cabbage, raisins and water or vegetable broth. Season with salt and white pepper and stir. Close the lid.

Stovetop: Set to high pressure (15 PSI) and cook over high heat for 7 minutes total.

Electric: Set to high pressure (10–12 PSI) and 7 minutes.

When done, turn off the heat or turn off the cooker and allow the pressure to release on its own (natural-release), about 3 minutes. If the pressure has not fully released after 3 minutes, apply auto-release. Open the cooker. If there is too much liquid, drain it.

Serve immediately.

Everyday Sweet Corn Purée

You'll be delighted with the layers of flavor this simple corn dish offers. The ancho chile powder adds an unexpected punch and is concentrated in those few minutes of cook time. I mentioned it earlier in the book, but I just love eating this with the Spicy Ancho Chile and Cilantro Short Ribs on page 59. The pairing is coherent and beautiful.

Serves 4 to 6

3 cups (450 g) fresh corn kernels, divided
¾ cup (175 ml) heavy whipping cream
¼ cup (120 ml) water
1 heaping tsp (6 g) sugar
1 tbsp (14 g) unsalted butter
½ tsp ancho chile powder
1 tsp (6 g) salt, or to taste
1 to 2 roasted piquillo peppers, sliced (optional)

Add 2 cups (300 g) of the corn kernels and the cream, water and sugar to a food processor. Pulse on medium speed until most of the corn has broken down and is mostly smooth, about 30 seconds. Add the butter and ancho chile powder to the pressure cooker. Melt over medium-low heat for the stovetop pressure cooker, or use the simmer setting for the electric pressure cooker, about 2 minutes. Add the pulsed corn mixture and stir well. Season with the salt. Cancel cooking for the electric cooker, and close the lid.

Stovetop: Set to low pressure (8 PSI) and cook over high heat for 5 minutes total.

Electric: Set to low pressure (5–8 PSI) and 7 minutes.

When done, turn off the heat or cancel cooking and allow the pressure to release on its own (natural-release), about 3 minutes. Stir in the remaining cup (150 g) of corn. Cook over medium heat for the stovetop cooker, or use the sauté setting for the electric cooker, and bring to a light boil, stirring occasionally using a whisk, about 3 minutes or until the purée thickens up a bit.

Serve immediately. Top with sliced *piquillo* peppers, if desired.

 B'S COOKING TIP: For a creamier and silkier purée, slowly stir in more cream and butter, to your desired texture. Keep in mind that adding more liquid can potentially flavor down the smoky corn taste. Adjust with ancho chile powder.

Cheesy Broccoli and Mushroom Casserole

Give a vintage American classic casserole an upgrade with panko and gourmet mushrooms. The texture of the broccoli is so perfectly achieved in the cooker, you'll never microwave it again.

Serves 4 to 6

3 tbsp (42 g) butter, plus more for baking dish

3 tbsp (22 g) all-purpose flour

1 tsp (1 g) dried thyme

½ tsp paprika

1 cup (151 g) diced Spanish onion

2 cloves garlic, minced

2 stalks celery, diced

5 cups (350 g) stemmed and sliced mixed wild mushrooms

2 heads broccoli, divided into florets

3 cups (345 g) shredded extra-sharp cheddar cheese

1 cup (235 ml) Herbed Chicken Stock (page 166), or store-bought

1½ cups (355 ml) heavy whipping cream

1 tsp (6 g) salt

⅛ tsp freshly ground white pepper

¼ cup (30 g) panko bread crumbs

Preheat the oven to 450°F (230°C). Warm the butter in the stovetop pressure cooker over medium heat, or use the sauté setting for the electric pressure cooker. Stir in the flour to create a roux-like mixture, about 1 minute. Cancel cooking for the electric cooker and use the residual heat to continue cooking. Add the thyme, paprika, onion, garlic, celery and mushrooms and cook for 2 minutes. Add the broccoli, 2 cups (230 g) of the cheese, the chicken stock and cream. Season with the salt and pepper. Stir to combine all of the ingredients and close the lid.

Stovetop: Set to high pressure (15 PSI) and cook over high heat for 8 minutes total.

Electric: Set to low pressure (5–8 PSI) and 6 minutes.

When done, remove the stovetop cooker from the heat and transfer to the sink to release the pressure, applying quick-release, or turn off the electric cooker and apply auto-release. When all of the pressure is out, open the cooker. Using a slotted spoon, transfer the mixture to an oven-safe, butter-coated baking dish. Top with the remaining cup (115 g) of cheese, followed by the panko crumbs. You can add an extra layer of cheese if you'd like. Place in the oven, uncovered, and bake for 15 minutes, or until the crumbs are nice and toasty. Alternatively, you can preheat your broiler to 300°F (150°C) and broil for a few minutes, but no more than 2 to 3 minutes. Remove from the oven and serve.

B'S COOKING TIP: I also made this dish using the mushroom stock remnants from the Wild Mushroom Velouté recipe on page 165. It's a great way of using everything in the kitchen and not being wasteful. The mushroom stems retain nutrients and flavor, too. Add with the whole mushrooms.

Southern Collard Greens with Smoked Turkey

My first real love was from southern Virginia, where soul food is the beloved food culture. I learned so much about American Southern cuisine from his mother. She used to make collard greens on Sunday morning, but I recall how tired she'd be from standing at the sink and working in earnest to trick the greens into cooking faster. Dinnertime was always based on the collard greens' behavior. I was so naive, but her pot of greens was simply divine. That was 24 years ago. This 40-minute recipe is strong, bold, nostalgic and outright smoky. The necks are the star this time. This recipe is for Ms. Annie Bell.

Serves 8 to 10

1½ tbsp (22 ml) canola oil

1 yellow onion, chopped

4 cloves garlic, mashed

1 smoked turkey neck

1 smoked turkey wing

4 cups (950 ml) water

1 tbsp (18 g) kosher salt

1 large bunch collard greens or about 17 leaves, stemmed and cut into 3" to 4" (7.5- to 10-cm) pieces

1 red or yellow bell pepper, cut into ½" (1.3-cm) julienne

1 tsp (5 ml) white distilled or cider vinegar (optional)

1 tsp (2.5 g) paprika (optional)

1 tsp (5 ml) Tabasco sauce

¼ tsp freshly ground black pepper

Heat the canola oil in the stovetop pressure cooker over medium heat, or use the sauté setting for the electric cooker. Add the onions, garlic, turkey neck and wing. Cook, stirring and not allowing the neck or wing to stick to the bottom of the cooker, about 1 minute. Add the water and salt, and stir.

Stovetop: Bring to a boil, over medium heat, about 5 minutes. Then reduce heat to low.

Electric: Maintain the sauté setting and bring to a boil, about 5 minutes. When done, cancel cooking.

Add the collard greens and bell pepper and stir to combine well. Vinegar and paprika are used in some super-classic collard greens recipes I've had over the years. If you'd like to modify with either one of these ingredients, add them here. Wait about 1 minute, then close the lid.

Stovetop: Set to high pressure (15 PSI) and set the timer for 30 minutes. Cook over high heat until pressure is reached, then lower heat to medium and continue cooking until done.

Electric: Set to high pressure (10–12 PSI) and 35 minutes.

When done, remove from heat or turn the cooker off and release the pressure using natural-release, about 6 to 10 minutes. If the pressure has not fully released after 10 minutes, apply auto-release. Stir in the Tabasco sauce, then season with ground black pepper. Adjust for salt. The meat on the bones will be tender and most of it will fall off.

Using tongs, remove the turkey neck and wings and pull any remaining meat off the bones and set aside. If, for your taste, there is too much liquid, strain as desired or reduce over medium-low heat. Add the meat back to the cooker and stir. Transfer to a serving platter and enjoy.

Bacon Lovers' Brussels Sprouts

It's a good moment in food culture when relatively unloved vegetables take a turn and become more than trendy. They transcend that phase and become part of the constant repertoire. In that case, Brussels sprouts come to mind. Their accessibility and ease in cooking, not to mention their pretty structure, put them in more and more unsuspecting plates. I added butter and fatty bacon to this recipe as a really inviting option for weekend brunch.

Serves 4 to 6

½ lb (225 g) sliced bacon, cut into ½" (1.3-cm) cubes

1–1½ tbsp (15–22 ml) olive oil

1½ lb (680 g) medium Brussels sprouts, trimmed and cut in half lengthwise

5 cups (550 g) evenly sized mixed baby potatoes medley, sliced in half lengthwise

1 medium red onion, cut into ½" (1.3-cm) julienne

1 tbsp (14 g) unsalted butter

¼ cup (60 ml) Herbed Chicken Stock (page 166), or store-bought

1 tsp (6 g) kosher salt or to taste

⅛ tsp freshly ground black pepper

Heat the stovetop pressure cooker over high or use the browning setting for the electric pressure cooker, and add the bacon. Cook for about 5 minutes, enough to render some fat. Lower the heat on the stovetop pressure cooker or cancel the browning setting for the electric pressure cooker and drain the bacon, transferring to a bowl and leaving the rendered bacon oil in the cooker. Add the olive oil and deglaze, scraping up any browned bacon bits. Add the Brussels sprouts. Cook over high heat in the stovetop pressure cooker or use the browning setting again for the electric pressure cooker, stirring occasionally, until most of the sprouts are lightly browned, about 3 minutes. Return the bacon to the pressure cooker and stir. Lower the heat to medium for the stovetop cooker, or cancel cooking for the electric cooker. Add the potatoes, onion and butter and stir. Pour in the chicken stock and season with the salt and pepper. Close the lid.

Stovetop: Set to high pressure (15 PSI) and cook over high heat for 7 to 8 minutes total.

Electric: Set to high pressure (10–12 PSI) and 3 minutes.

When done, remove the stovetop cooker from the heat and transfer to the sink to release the pressure with a quick-release, or turn off the electric cooker and apply auto-release. When all of the pressure is out, adjust for salt and transfer to your serving dish.

 B'S COOKING TIP: Make sure your sprouts and potatoes are roughly the same size. And, depending on both their sizes, you may wish to leave smaller ones whole and cook a little longer, up to 2 minutes, with the pressure cooker covered but without pressure.

NO PRESSURE! DESSERTS

One of the most rewarding successes I've enjoyed in the last ten years has been introducing the pressure cooker and its art to anyone who's been willing to listen and learn. If people have gone as far as purchasing a pressure cooker and letting me know how much they love it, I'm really successful! I know of about 80 to date. It means my argument for owning one and my publicly shared recipes are enticing. Second to that has been convincing people that desserts are very doable in this classic vessel. It all started with making a decadent espresso flan in a 60-year-old cooker. I shared that flan on my blog, Flanboyant Eats, in 2008 and the reaction was humbling. So many of my readers were pleasantly shocked. They had no idea a lovely and ultracreamy crème caramel could be made in grandma's antique pot. I'm excited to share four of those flan recipes in this chapter. The other desserts in here are lovely options for year-round and holiday enjoyment as well. You will love the fluffiness, creaminess, sweetness and silky texture each one offers. The Tangy Candied Orange Shells recipe (page 189) is a great example of how to make use of everything in your kitchen. The Luscious Lemon Chiffon Cheesecake with Blueberry Coulis (page 203) is my second favorite. Don't be afraid to explore and test. Really. And if you dare, eat dessert first. With good espresso, of course.

Provençal Mixed Fruit Compote with Wine and Elderflower

I spent three weeks in France celebrating a milestone birthday with the sole purpose of exploring all I could about its rich culinary flair. A quaint, hole-in-the-wall bistro, à la Americano, about one block from Château de Valençay, where I had just spent two hours, shared with me a fluffy cake smothered with a warm fruit compote and crème fraîche. It was heavenly. I've made a version of that compote during the holidays since then, inspired by my affinity for Champagne, with a splash of elderflower liqueur and the abundant use of cloves in some of my staple savory dishes. This quick cook-down is a decadent and romantic fruit mixture to enjoy with a moist cake or ice cream, or on its own. It makes me want to go back.

SERVES 6

½ cup (73 g) fresh blueberries

2 medium peaches, pitted and quartered

1 cup (150 g) Champagne grapes

1 Bosc pear, peeled, cored and cut into 2"
(5-cm) chunks

1 cup (200 g) sugar

1 tsp (5 ml) pure vanilla extract

1 cinnamon stick

½ tsp ground cardamom

3 whole cloves

Pinch of salt

1 cup (120 ml) dry white wine

1 cup (120 ml) sweet red wine (Marsala is
a good option)

1 tbsp (15 ml) water

2 cups (300 g) fresh strawberries, hulled
and halved lengthwise

Juice of 1 lemon (reserve peel for garnish)

2 tbsp (30 ml) elderflower liqueur

½ cup (78 g) frozen blueberries

1 tbsp (1.5 g) culinary-grade lavender
flowers

Fresh basil, chopped, for garnish (optional)

Add all of the ingredients to the pressure cooker, except the strawberries, lemon peel and juice, elderflower liqueur, frozen blueberries, lavender flowers and basil leaves. Gently stir and close the lid.

Stovetop: Set to high pressure (15 PSI) and cook over high heat for 4 minutes total.

Electric: Set to high pressure (10–12 PSI) and 2 minutes.

When done, remove from the heat or cancel the cooker and allow the pressure to release on its own (natural-release), about 10 to 12 minutes. When all of the pressure is out, remove the fruit with a slotted spoon and transfer to a large bowl. Stir the strawberries and lemon juice into the cooker. Reduce the syrup over medium-high heat for the stovetop pressure cooker or using the sauté setting for the electric pressure cooker, until the syrup is lightly thickened, about 5 to 6 minutes. When done, remove from the heat or turn off the cooker. Stir in the elderflower liqueur and frozen blueberries. Pour into a bowl with the fruits, and gently stir.

Sprinkle the lavender flowers all over. Serve over vanilla ice cream and garnish with fresh basil and lemon peel.

Store for up to 5 days.

 B'S COOKING TIP: A good wine substitution I've tried and really enjoy, for the dry white and Marsala, is equal parts Viognier (white) and Syrah (red).

BRANDY-GLAZED PEARS WITH PINEAPPLE AND GINGER

My mother has a sweet tooth sweeter than a piece of hard candy. She loves sweets in all forms. The most inspiring *dulce* moments for me are when she asks me to indulge and treat her to something sweet but longer lasting. Something you can store and go back to. I created this years back when she showed up with a bag of fresh fruits and asked me to "just figure it out!" This sexy and warm bowl of softened fruit and slow-streaming herbed syrup is part her palate, part my vision of a perfect fall dessert with coffee or a sip of Grand Marnier. This pairs well with ice cream, cream cheese slices or rum cake.

SERVES 6

4 Bosc pears, peeled, cored and sliced into 2" (2.5-cm) slices

3 cups (510 g) pineapple, cut into 1½" (3.8-cm) chunks

1 cup (220 g) brown sugar, packed

½ cup (120 ml) water

3 tbsp (24 g) grated fresh ginger

1 tsp (2 g) ground nutmeg

Pinch of salt

⅓ cup (89 ml) French brandy or Grand Marnier

1 star anise, whole (optional)

Add all of the ingredients, except the brandy, to the pressure cooker and stir. Close the lid.

Stovetop: Set to high pressure (15 PSI) and cook over high heat until it reaches pressure, about 3 to 4 minutes, then turn the heat off.

Electric: Set to high pressure (10–12 PSI) and 4 minutes.

When done, remove from the heat or turn off the cooker and allow the pressure to release on its own (natural-release), about 4 to 5 minutes. When all of the pressure is out, open the cooker. Stir in the brandy and lightly reduce the sauce over low heat for 10 minutes for the stovetop pressure cooker or using the simmer setting for the electric pressure cooker, until it has thickened to your desired consistency. It should not be too runny or so thick that you have to add liquid.

Serve warm.

 B'S COOKING TIP: Soak the pears in brandy for 20 minutes before cooking. This is optional, but yields a really smooth taste.

TANGY CANDIED ORANGE SHELLS

The Orange Marmalade recipe on page 206 birthed this new dessert! Not being wasteful comes to life in this tangy treat made of orange shells we'd naturally throw away. This simple dessert is really tasty with soft Brie. Vanilla bean ice cream or lemon sorbet pairs well, too, especially with the syrup drizzled over the top. Delight your guests with this bright treat.

SERVES 4 TO 6

Peeled shells from 3 oranges, skinned of most of their pith and halved

2 whole cloves

2 whole star anise

2 cups (475 ml) water

¾ cup plus 2 tbsp (167 g) white or cane sugar

Pinch of salt

2 tbsp (28 ml) Grand Marnier or other good quality orange liqueur

1 tbsp (9 g) orange zest

Freshly grated nutmeg, for garnish (optional)

Add the orange shells, cloves, star anise, water, sugar and salt to the pressure cooker and stir. Close the lid.

Stovetop: Set to high pressure (15 PSI) and cook over medium-high heat for 15 minutes total.

Electric: Set to high pressure (10–12 PSI) and 25 minutes.

When done, remove from the heat or cancel cooking and allow the pressure to release on its own (natural-release), about 6 to 8 minutes. When all of the pressure is out, remove the orange shells with a slotted spoon and transfer to a large glass serving bowl. The consistency of the syrup in the cooker should be that of agave. If it's not, bring to a boil over medium heat for the stovetop cooker or using the sauté setting for the electric pressure cooker, about 5 to 7 minutes or until the syrup reaches your desired consistency. Gently stir in the Grand Marnier. Pour the syrup over the shells.

Sprinkle with the orange zest and ground nutmeg. Serve warm or cold.

B'S COOKING TIP: One fun way to serve this is to fill the orange shells with ice cream. To do so, strain and reserve the syrup in a bowl. Evenly place the shells on a baking sheet. Cover and freeze for 10 to 15 minutes, enough to chill the shells. Remove and add 1 to 2 scoops of ice cream to the each shell. Pour the warm syrup over the top and enjoy! You can add orange zest and nutmeg as well.

THE FLAN

I am certain most people aren't aware flan is said to have origins in Rome during the Napoleonic era. Peasants' lack of resources and food nurtured a spirit of ingenuity with the little they did have. Eggs and milk were boiled on top of a wood fire to make a custardlike dish. Modern accounts credit Mexicans with inventing it. However, Cubans have a known trait for claiming to be the mother of all goodness, including and especially flan.

My affinity for flan was born out of my mother's tease. Growing up, she'd treat the family to one every blue moon. My dad's ration was three-quarters of one whole flan, while my siblings and I had to fight over scraps. Having the pressure cooker on my side, I set out to conquer her luxurious crème caramel. When I did, I lost my mind. With 50 flavor combinations to date, there's no doubt this is my favorite kitchen experiment. When done right, flan is a simple egg custard bearing a silky texture and sexy cognac-colored liquid caramel. It's intoxicating. Traditionally stovetop cooking or baking in a bain-marie takes up to 90 minutes. In my precious pressure cookers, whether vintage, stovetop or electric, it takes no more than 20 minutes; some even as little as ten. Those short times will invite any novice to play around and craft mind-blowing flavor profiles.

Chef-of-the-Century Joël Robuchon enjoyed one of my classic vanilla flans one afternoon while I was visiting in his former atelier in New York. His reaction: "Bren, ooh-la-la. This is the perfect crème caramel for young and old. It's the perfect dessert." He and his team ate it all.

Enjoy these four flans, ranging from basic to a little more elaborate. All are decadent. Just be ready for your kitchen to smell like a caramel factory. For more information on flans and how the use of different ingredients affects the egg-to-milk ratio and cooking time, visit my site BrenHerrera.com.

— B'S COOKING TIP —

Inserting and Removing the Flan Mold

A flan mold, commonly known as a *flanera*, makes life so much easier when making flan and other round desserts. Having a secure lid allows you to safely and securely place the dessert in the cooker without incident. Taking it out can be another story. I always use thick kitchen towels or my silicone gloves to safely remove anything from the cooker. I'm okay with that. I'd suggest you use the same caution too, if you're comfortable enough (or tall enough!) to place your covered hands in the hot pressure cooker.

However, if you don't have super-heat-resistant gloves (up to 500°F [260°C]) or simply feel better pulling out your flan mold in a less intrusive way, make a makeshift "handle" with aluminum foil. Place the mold over a 12-inch (30.5-cm) piece of aluminum foil. Twist the sides of the foil until you have handles long enough to grip. Use this to lower into or remove from the cooker a flan mold or anything of the like you're using.

THE EASIEST CLASSIC VANILLA FLAN

All flans are built from this basic one. Some make it with four eggs and evaporated milk. This combination is the perfect one I settled on over fifteen years ago. As basic as it is, it's subtly rich and a lovely canvas to top with anything you like.

SERVES 6

3 large eggs, at room temperature

1 (14-oz [425-ml]) can sweetened condensed milk

14 oz (425 ml) whole milk

1 tsp (5 ml) pure vanilla extract

2 sprigs rosemary, 1 finely minced and 1 whole (optional)

6 tbsp (78 g) cane sugar

B'S COOKING TIPS:
Some flans, depending on the ingredients, will need 4 large eggs. If the flan is a bit jiggly when you remove it from the cooker, place it back in the stovetop pressure cooker and set to high pressure for 2 more minutes over high heat or set to high pressure for the electric pressure cooker. When done, release the pressure, applying a quick-release.

In a medium mixing bowl, stir the eggs, using a wire whisk. Whisk in the sweetened condensed milk, followed by the whole milk, vanilla and finely minced rosemary, without creating bubbles, about 1 minute. Set aside.

To a round 1-quart (946-ml) aluminum flan mold or pan, add the sugar and place on the burner. Turn the heat to high and begin caramelizing the sugar, stirring constantly. Reduce the heat to medium-high as soon as it starts to melt, using a wooden spoon or medium silicone spatula, 2 to 5 minutes, until the sugar is completely melted and beautifully golden.

Turn off and remove the mold immediately from the heat. Working fast, coat the entire mold with the melted sugar, rotating it in a controlled circular motion. If you are not experienced in handling extremely hot caramel, leave the mold on your counter and quickly coat with a pastry brush or a small silicone spatula. It is about 330°F (165°C) at this point. Set aside and let sit until the caramel sets, about 1 minute. Pour the custard mixture into the flan mold, using a medium-mesh hand strainer to collect the egg embryo. This last step here is not entirely necessary.

Add enough water to the pressure cooker to cover the mold at least halfway. Close the flan mold or cover your pan with aluminum foil and gently place in the middle of the cooker. Close the lid.

Stovetop: Set to high pressure (15 PSI) and set the timer for 15 minutes. Cook over high heat until the pressure is reached, about 10 minutes, then turn off the heat but do not remove the cooker from the stove. The residual heat will finish cooking it. Allow the pressure to release on its own for the remaining 5 minutes.

Electric: Set to high pressure (10–12 PSI) and 15 minutes. When done, cancel cooking. Allow the pressure to release on its own (natural-release).

When all of the pressure is out, open the cooker and gently remove the mold, using silicone gloves. Do not unmold. Chill the flan for at least 5 hours, giving it enough time to set. 8 hours is ideal. Remove the flan from the fridge 30 minutes prior to serving. To unmold, open the flan mold and loosen the sides, using a butter knife. Place a large plate on top of the mold and gently but quickly flip upside down. Allow all of the liquid caramel to drizzle all over the flan. Try not to waste any of this liquid gold! Garnish with fresh rosemary, if desired.

DECADENT ESPRESSO AND TOASTED ALMOND FLAN

A perfect marriage of two of the very things that represent my love of food and culture: espresso and flan. It doesn't get much better than this. The toasty almonds add great texture and the espresso will subtly keep you energized.

SERVES 6 TO 8

4 large eggs, at room temperature

1 (14-oz [425-ml]) can sweetened condensed milk

14 oz (425 ml) whole milk

¾ cup (175 ml) plus 1 tbsp (180 ml) unsweetened brewed espresso

1 tsp (5 ml) pure vanilla extract

1 tsp (5 ml) almond extract

½ tsp espresso salt

½ cup (100 g) cane sugar

½ cup (73 g) toasted almonds, sliced, for garnish

Ground espresso, for garnish

In a medium mixing bowl, stir the eggs, using a wire whisk. Whisk in the sweetened condensed milk, followed by the whole milk, ¾ cup (175 ml) of the brewed espresso, the extracts and the espresso salt. Whisk until all of the ingredients are well-blended, without creating bubbles, about 1 minute. Set aside.

To a round 1-quart (946-ml) aluminum flan mold or pan, add the sugar and the remaining tablespoon (15 ml) of brewed espresso and place on the burner. Turn the heat to high and begin caramelizing the sugar, stirring constantly. Reduce the heat to medium-high as soon as it starts to melt, using a wooden spoon or medium silicone spatula, 2 to 5 minutes, until the sugar is completely melted and a beautiful golden Cognac color.

Turn off and remove the mold immediately from the heat. Working fast, coat the entire mold with the melted sugar, rotating it in a controlled circular motion. If you are not experienced in handling extremely hot caramel, leave the mold on your counter and quickly coat with a pastry brush or a small silicone spatula. It is about 330°F (165°C) at this point. Set aside and let sit until the caramel sets, about 1 minute. Pour the custard mixture into the flan mold or pan, using a medium-mesh hand strainer to collect the egg embryo. This last step here is not entirely necessary.

Add enough water to the cooker to cover the mold halfway. Close the mold or cover your pan with aluminum foil and gently place in the middle of the cooker. Close the lid.

Stovetop: Set to high pressure (15 PSI) and set the timer for 16 minutes. Cook over high heat until the pressure point is reached, about 11 minutes, then turn off the heat but do not remove the cooker from the stove. The residual heat will finish cooking it. Allow the pressure to release on its own for the remaining 5 to 6 minutes.

Electric: Set to high pressure (10–12 PSI) and 16 minutes. When done, cancel cooking. Allow the pressure to release on its own (natural-release).

When all of the pressure is out, open the cooker and gently remove the mold, using silicone gloves. Do not unmold. Chill the flan for at least 5 hours, giving it enough time to set. Remove the flan from the fridge 30 minutes prior to serving. See the directions on page 192 for tips on unmolding the flan. Garnish with almonds and ground espresso.

Toasted Pistachio and Cardamom Flan

This flan was inspired by a few different and recent trips around the world. I enjoyed a typical Israeli dessert, *malabi*, in Akko that was divine. It was dainty but full of character. The milk-based, rose-water pudding, topped with toasted pistachio, seems to be one of the locals' most beloved desserts. This flan reminds me of that dainty dessert I so thoroughly enjoyed in a rustic Arab fishing village.

Serves 6 to 8

½ cup (73 g) pistachios, whole, plus 3 tbsp (27 g) crushed, for garnish

1 tbsp (13 g) salted butter

1 tsp (2 g) ground cardamom

3 large eggs, at room temperature

1 (14-oz [425-ml]) can sweetened condensed milk

14 oz (425 ml) whole milk

1 tsp (5 ml) pure vanilla extract

6 tbsp (78 ml) cane sugar

In a mortar, crush the pistachios until they are micro-sized crumbles. In a small skillet, warm the butter and toast the pistachios with the cardamom, over medium heat, stirring constantly, about 3 minutes. Transfer to a small bowl and set aside. In a medium mixing bowl, stir the eggs, using a wire whisk. Whisk in the sweetened condensed milk, followed by the whole milk, vanilla and pistachio mixture, without creating bubbles, about 1 minute. Set aside.

To a round 1-quart (946-ml) aluminum flan mold or pan, add the sugar and place on the burner. Turn the heat to high and begin caramelizing the sugar, stirring constantly. Reduce the heat to medium-high as soon as it starts to melt, using a wooden spoon or medium silicone spatula, 2 to 5 minutes, until the sugar is completely melted and beautifully golden.

Turn off and remove the mold immediately from the heat. Working fast, coat the entire mold with the melted sugar, rotating it in a controlled circular motion. If you are not experienced in handling extremely hot caramel, leave the mold on your counter and quickly coat with a pastry brush or a small silicone spatula. The sugar is about 330°F (165°C) at this point. Set aside and let sit until the caramel sets, about 1 minute. Pour the custard mixture into the flan mold or pan using a medium-mesh hand strainer to collect the egg embryo. This last step here is not entirely necessary.

Add enough water to the cooker to cover the mold halfway. Close the mold or cover the pan with aluminum foil and place in the middle of the cooker. Close the lid.

Stovetop: Set to high pressure (15 PSI) and set the timer for 17 minutes. Cook over high heat until the pressure point is reached, about 12 minutes, then turn off the heat but do not remove the cooker from the stove. The residual heat will finish cooking it. Allow the pressure to release on its own for the remaining 5 minutes.

Electric: Set to high pressure (10–12 PSI) and 15 minutes. When done, cancel cooking. Allow the pressure to release on its own (natural-release).

When all of the pressure is out, open the cooker and gently remove the mold, using silicone gloves. Do not unmold. Chill for at least 5 hours, giving it enough time to set. Remove the flan from the fridge 30 minutes prior to serving. See the directions on page 192 for tips on unmolding the flan. Garnish with additional pistachios.

BLACK TRUFFLE AND THYME FLAN

Some of my flans caught the attention of a celebrity chef in Melbourne in 2012. The Tourism Office in Victoria partnered with an agency in New York to host a recipe contest. I was asked to submit a recipe featuring anything that comes from the earth. I submitted my truffle and thyme flan, and after a very palm-sweating dinner event in TriBeCa, Chef Guy said he loved my flan the best. I had won! The prize was a trip to Australia's Food and Wine Festival. I've relished the right moment to share this recipe with you.

YIELDS 3 OR 4 INDIVIDUAL RAMEKINS

Custard

3 large eggs, at room temperature

1 (16-oz [475-ml]) can sweetened condensed milk

½ cup (120 ml) whole milk

1 tsp (5 g) vanilla bean seeds, scraped from the pod

½ tsp pure vanilla extract

Leaves from 2 sprigs thyme

3 to 4 slices black truffle, minced, plus more, sliced, for garnish

Caramel

8 tbsp (78 g) muscovado sugar

Pinch of black truffle salt

2 tbsp (28 ml) water

Prepare the custard: In a medium mixing bowl, stir the eggs, using a wire whisk. Whisk in the sweetened condensed milk, followed by the whole milk, vanilla bean seeds, vanilla extract, thyme and minced truffles, about 1 minute. Set aside.

Prepare the caramel: Have ready 3 or 4 individual ramekins, depending on the size of your cooker. Add the sugar, truffle salt and water to an 8-inch (20.5-cm) nonstick skillet and place on the burner. Using a wooden spoon, stir and caramelize over high heat. When the sugar starts to caramelize and begins to turn a golden, Cognac color, lower the heat to medium-high and stir constantly until fully melted, about 2 minutes. Turn off the heat and remove the skillet immediately from the burner. Working fast, pour enough caramel into a ramekin and coat all around, rotating it in a controlled circular motion. (Use 2 to 4 tablespoons [30 to 40 ml], depending on size of ramekin. The idea is to coat the entire ramekin but with not too thick a layer. This may take some practice!) Quickly move on to the next ramekin and repeat. Use a brush if you are not experienced in handling extremely hot caramel. It is about 330°F (165°C) at this point. Continue until all of the ramekins are coated. Evenly distribute the custard mixture into the coated ramekins and fill to the top of the caramel. Cover each ramekin with aluminum foil.

Add enough water to the pressure cooker to cover the ramekins halfway. Gently place the ramekins in the middle of the cooker. Close the lid.

Stovetop: Set to high pressure (15 PSI) and set the timer for 13 minutes. Cook over high heat until the pressure point is reached, about 10 minutes, then turn off the heat but do not remove the cooker from the stove. The residual heat will finish cooking the flans. Allow all of the pressure to release on its own for the remaining 3 minutes.

Electric: Set to high pressure (10–12 PSI) and 15 minutes. When done, cancel cooking. Allow the pressure to release on its own (natural-release).

When all of the pressure is out, open the cooker and gently remove the ramekins, using silicone gloves. Do not unmold. Chill for at least 5 hours, giving them enough time to set. Remove the flans from the fridge 30 minutes prior to serving. See page 192 for tips on unmolding the flan. Garnish each individual flan with sliced truffle and fresh thyme.

BLUEBERRY ALMOND JAM

The following jam recipes are a delight to make in the pressure cooker as they save you nearly one hour in comparison to a conventional slow simmer which can easily climb to two and a half hours. This blueberry and almond jam blends so well you'll end up using it as a smooth topping for other desserts. I eat it with ice cream, Greek yogurt and toast, of course. Imagine it on crusty corn bread!

YIELDS 6 CUPS (1.9 KG) JAM

2 lbs or 2¾ cups (905 g) fresh blueberries

4 cups (800 g) sugar

Juice of 1 lemon

½ cup (120 ml) water

1 tsp (5 ml) almond extract

5–7 fresh basil leaves, finely minced

Place a small glass plate in the freezer. This is how we're going to test the doneness of the jam. Add all of the ingredients to the pressure cooker and stir. Close the lid.

Stovetop: Set to high pressure (15 PSI) and set the timer for 60 minutes. Cook over high heat until the pressure point has been reached, then lower the heat enough to maintain high pressure, and continue to cook.

Electric: Set to high pressure (10–12 PSI) and 70 minutes.

When done, remove from the heat or turn off the cooker and allow the pressure to release on its own (natural-release), about 15 minutes. When all of the pressure is out, open the cooker.

If using a stovetop pressure cooker, keep the cooker uncovered and bring to a boil over high heat; for the electric pressure cooker, use the sauté setting and bring to a boil. Reduce the heat to medium or cancel the sauté setting and reset to the simmer setting; cook for 5 to 7 minutes, or until the jam is reduced to a consistency of spreadable jam.

To test for doneness, remove the glass plate from the freezer and add a dollop of the blueberry jam to it. After 1 minute, check for doneness. If the jam has settled in place, it's done. If it's runny, it needs more time to set. Continue to cook, about 10 minutes over high heat. When done, remove from the heat. Transfer to mason jars and allow to cool before closing. Chill until ready to serve.

This jam can last for up to 1 year.

STRAWBERRY GINGER JAM

Pressure cookers are also great for canning certain fruits and vegetables. Historically, they were used to can jams. For instant enjoyment, you can simply make a wild range of jams, jellies and spreads in the cooker, without having to figure out how canning works. This strawberry ginger jam is my way of lusting over one of my favorite commercial brands I only buy when I'm in a superpinch. But then again, if I make a large-enough batch, I should always have enough to enjoy whenever my cravings kick in. Try this with raspberries, too!

YIELDS 6 CUPS (1.9 KG) JAM

2 lbs (905 g) fresh strawberries, hulled

1 lemon

2 tbsp (12 g) grated fresh ginger

4 cups (800 g) sugar

¼ cup (60 ml) freshly squeezed orange juice

Place a small glass plate in the freezer. This is how we're going to test the doneness of the jam. Wash and cut the strawberries into quarters. Add all of the ingredients to the pressure cooker and stir. Close the lid.

Stovetop: Set to high pressure (15 PSI) and set the timer for 60 minutes. Cook over high heat until the pressure point has been reached, then lower the heat enough to maintain high pressure, and continue to cook.

Electric: Set to high pressure (10–12 PSI) and 60 minutes.

When done, remove from the heat or turn off the cooker and allow the pressure to release on its own (natural-release), about 15 minutes. When all of the pressure is out, open the cooker.

If using a stovetop pressure cooker, bring to a boil over high heat; for the electric pressure cooker, use the sauté setting and bring to a boil. Reduce the heat to low or cancel the sauté setting and reset to the simmer setting; cook for 10 minutes, or until the jam is reduced to a consistency of spreadable jam.

To test for doneness, remove the glass plate from the freezer and add a dollop of the strawberry jam. After 1 minute, check for doneness. If the jam has settled in place, it's done. If it's runny, it needs more time to set. Continue to cook, about 10 minutes, over high heat. When done, remove from the heat. Transfer to mason jars and allow to cool before closing. Chill until ready to serve.

This jam can last for up to 1 year.

Luscious Lemon Chiffon Cheesecake with Blueberry Coulis

My mother and sister are cheesecake fanatics. My father used to make my mother a really rich one every time she put in a request. He stopped making them for her at some point; or she just moved on to something else. Her thing these days is crème brûlée. Meanwhile, my sister goes out to buy her cheesecake. As for me, I've never really been a huge fan. I always found them to be entirely too sweet and densely rich. I challenged myself to change our respective experiences. I made this so that my mother could see how incredibly easy she can make it to her own liking. My sister, the natural baker in the family, will eventually just make it for herself, too. I've just started getting my sister into pressure cooking. This will seal the deal. And I finally found a consistency and sweet level I actually like. The added hint of limoncello brightens it more.

A deep 6-inch (15-cm) diameter springform cake pan is ideal for this recipe. I've also used a standard 7-inch (18-cm) diameter mold and it was fine, only lower in height.

SERVES 6

Cheesecake

2 cups (144 g) crushed graham crackers

½ cup (120 ml) plus 2 tsp (10 ml) melted butter

1 lb (455 g) cream cheese, softened

1 (16-oz [455-ml]) can sweetened condensed milk

3 large eggs, at room temperature

Juice and zest of 1 lemon, plus 1½ tbsp (13.5 g) lemon zest

½ cup (100 g) sugar

1 tsp (5 ml) pure vanilla extract

1½ tsp (7.5 ml) lemon extract

½ tsp salt

Blueberry Coulis

3 tbsp (45 ml) limoncello

1 cup Blueberry Almond Jam (page 200)

½ cup (75 g) fresh blueberries

Lemon peel (optional)

Prepare the cheesecake: In a mini food processor, pulse the graham crackers until finely crumbled, about 2 minutes. Transfer to a mixing bowl and add the ½ cup (120 ml) of melted butter. Stir well. Evenly coat the bottom of your cake pan or mold with the remaining 2 teaspoons (10 ml) of melted butter. Then spread out the graham cracker crumble in the pan, patting it down with the back of a spoon or your fingers. Place the mold in the fridge while you make the batter. This will set the crust and keep it from floating once you add the batter.

In a stand mixer or a large bowl using a hand mixer, combine the cream cheese and sweetened condensed milk. Beat for 2 to 3 minutes, until smooth with no clumps. Occasionally scrape the sides of the bowl to get any cream cheese. Add the eggs, one by one, and continue to mix on the second speed. Add the lemon juice and continue to mix for a few more seconds. Stop the mixer and add the sugar, extracts, the zest of 1 lemon and the salt. Turn the mixer back on to the second speed and beat or mix until the batter is really smooth, about 2 more minutes, ensuring not to overbeat.

Remove the cake pan from the fridge. Gently pour the cream cheese batter into the mold and spread out evenly, using a rubber spatula. Add 1 cup (120 ml) of water to the cooker. Place the cake pan over a 12-inch (30.5-cm) piece of aluminum foil. Twist the sides of the foil until you have "handles." Holding the "handles," gently lower the cake pan into the cooker. The water level should be halfway up the side of the cake pan. Close the lid.

(continued)

Luscious Lemon Chiffon Cheesecake with Blueberry Coulis (Cont.)

Stovetop: Set to high pressure (15 PSI) and cook over medium-high heat for 18 minutes total.

Electric: Set to high pressure (10–12 PSI) and 20 to 22 minutes.

When done, remove from the heat or turn off the cooker and allow the pressure to release on its own (natural-release), about 4 to 5 minutes. If the pressure is not out after 5 minutes, apply auto-release. When all of the pressure is out, open the cooker and gently remove the cake pan, using the foil "handles." Place the pan on a cooling rack and let cool for 30 minutes. Cover with foil, leaving room between the cake and the foil, and chill for at least 4 hours so that it sets nicely.

Prepare the blueberry coulis: Add the limoncello to the blueberry jam. Stir to mix well. Add the fresh blueberries. Gently mash the blueberries while stirring with a wooden spoon, to create some volume and texture. When ready to enjoy, spread 1 cup (320 g) of the coulis over the top of the cheesecake. Finish off with remaining lemon zest. Garnish with lemon peel, if desired.

DELICIOUS APPLE AND KIWI SAUCE

As a stand-alone fruit, apples don't call my name much. Honey crisps are the only ones I can bite into, and even then, I have to be in the mood or have an unlikely craving. But I love apples in everything else! I love cider, I love pie, I love apple butter, I love apple bread, I love it all . . . as long as they're cooked. And funny enough, I don't like applesauce. But when your brother goes apple picking (an annual thing for him) and shows up with ten pounds (4.6 kg) of Red Delicious, you tweak it and make an amazing sauce. I can't think of a simpler dessert, topping or filling than this apple-kiwi sauce cooked in eight minutes. It's the easiest recipe in this cookbook.

YIELDS 8 CUPS (1.9 KG) SAUCE

3 lb (1.4 g) Red Delicious apples, peeled and cored

4 green kiwis, peeled and halved

1 tsp (2 g) ground cinnamon

1 tsp (5 ml) pure vanilla extract

1 cup (200 g) sugar

1½ cups (355 ml) water

Add all of the ingredients to the pressure cooker and stir. Close the lid.

Stovetop: Set to high pressure (15 PSI) and cook over high heat for 8 minutes total.

Electric: Set to high pressure (10–12 PSI) and 8 minutes.

When done, remove from the heat or turn off the cooker and allow the pressure to release on its own (natural-release), about 5 minutes. When all of the pressure is out, open the cooker and mash the fruits, using the back of a wooden spoon or potato masher, until all the fruit chunks are mostly smooth. Chill until ready to serve.

Will keep for up to 7 days, stored in glass jars.

ORANGE MARMALADE

I love New York so much I've considered moving there several times over the course of 20 years. It's not just the energy and vibe. It's also the food. In 1996 I walked into a super random *mercado* (street market) in Brooklyn to buy coffee and ended up perusing other aisles. I found this pretty jar with a French label reading "Marmelade d'Orange," so I bought it and made my way back to Charlottesville, where I was studying at UVA. I fell in love with that amazing bitter orange "jelly." But I was a broke college kid and $4.50 for jelly was not happening. I realized over time how much I love orange marmalade; I just want to make it for myself and store batches and batches worth. Sarabeth's in Central Park was the second-ever marmalade I've had since 1996. That was just two years ago. I finally decided to make my own version. This is one you can enjoy along with the two other jam recipes. A tasting of all three with a variety of breads and Brie cheese is a nice way to host your friends.

YIELDS 8 CUPS (2.6 KG) MARMALADE

6 large Florida oranges (4 lbs [1.8 kg]), peeled (reserve the peel) and halved

3 whole cloves

3 cups (710 ml) water

3 tbsp (18 g) pith (white part of orange peel), minced

3 cups (600 g) sugar

Peel from half of the whole oranges

¼ cup (24 g) of the remaining orange peel, thinly sliced in ½" (1.3-cm) lengths

2 tbsp (12 g) of the remaining orange peel, finely minced

Place a small glass plate in the freezer. This is how we're going to test the doneness of the jam.

Add all of the ingredients to the pressure cooker and stir. Close the lid.

Stovetop: Set to high pressure (15 PSI) and cook over high heat for 35 minutes total.

Electric: Set to high pressure (10–12 PSI) and 45 minutes.

When done, remove from the heat or cancel the cooker and allow the pressure to release on its own (natural-release). When all of the pressure is out, open the cooker.

Stovetop: Bring to a boil over high heat. Continue to cook over high heat for 5 minutes. Lower the heat to medium and simmer until the jam is reduced to your desired consistency, about 5 minutes.

Electric: Set to the simmer setting. Bring to a boil and cook for 10 minutes, or until the jam is reduced to your desired consistency. Check for doneness (see below). If not done after 10 minutes, transfer to a medium/large saucepan and bring to a boil for 5 minutes on the stove.

To check for doneness, remove the glass plate from the freezer and add a dollop of the orange marmalade to it. After 1 minute, if the jam has settled in place, it's done. If it's runny, it needs more time to set. Continue to cook, about 10 minutes, over high heat. When done, remove from the heat and discard the long orange peel before storing.

Transfer to mason jars and allow to cool before closing. Chill until ready to serve. Marmalade will keep for up to 4 months in the fridge.

ISLAND LEMON-LIME TAPIOCA

Did you know tapioca comes from cassava or yuca? It's no wonder it's such a smooth and creamy pudding-like treat. The pearls are hard to break down, but applying pressure softens them enough to make a light and fluffy bowl with citrus notes. This recipe is a bit laborious—I won't lie or pretend—but I promise the goodness is so worth it. It's too good not to try!

SERVES 4

¾ cup (114 g) pearl tapioca

2½ cups (590 ml) whole milk, divided

½ cup (120 ml) water

¼ cup (20 g) shredded coconut

½ cup (100 g) sugar

2 large egg yolks, lightly beaten

1 tsp (5 ml) lemon extract

⅛ tsp kosher salt

Zest from 1 lime

Add the tapioca, 2 cups (475 ml) of milk and the water to the pressure cooker. Stir and close the lid.

Stovetop: Set to high pressure (15 PSI) and cook over low-medium heat for 10 minutes total.

Electric: Set to high pressure (10–12 PSI) and 7 minutes.

When done, remove the stovetop cooker from the heat and allow the pressure to release on its own (natural-release) for 3 minutes, then apply auto-release, or turn off the electric cooker and apply slow auto-release (refer to page 19 if needed). When all of the pressure is out, open the cooker. Add the remaining ingredients, except for half of the lime zest.

Bring to a light boil over medium-low heat for the stovetop cooker or using the simmer setting for the electric cooker, stirring constantly with a wire whisk, about 5 minutes or until it thickens up.

Immediately transfer the pudding to a serving bowl. Allow the pudding to set, refrigerating it for at least 30 minutes. Dust with the remaining lime zest when serving.

SPICED AND CANDIED PAPAYA

Fruta Bomba

There are some things that just don't need fixing. *Fruta bomba* is a typical dessert we eat after dinner with a mildly firm slice of cream cheese. A really green papaya turns into a bowl of softened pieces smothered in a spiced and aromatic simple syrup. Star anise seeds, ginger and rosemary are my added spins to a nostalgic experience.

SERVES 6

1 cup (235 ml) water

2 cups (400 g) sugar

1 tsp (3 g) grated fresh ginger

1 tsp (2 g) star anise seeds

Pinch of salt

1 large green papaya (about 9" [13 cm] long), seeded and cut into 2" (5-cm) pieces

Leaves from 2 sprigs rosemary

Add all of the ingredients, except the papaya and half of the rosemary, to the pressure cooker and stir. Add the papaya and close the lid.

Stovetop: Set to high pressure (15 PSI) and cook over high heat for 10 minutes total.

Electric: Set to high pressure (10–12 PSI) and 10 minutes.

When done, remove from the heat or turn off the cooker and allow the pressure to release on its own (natural-release), about 5 to 7 minutes. When all of the pressure is out, open the cooker and gently transfer the fruit mixture to a glass serving dish, using a large slotted spoon. Pour or ladle the syrup over the top. Garnish with the remaining rosemary.

Serve this with semihardened cream cheese slices.

B'S COOKING TIPS: Make sure to get a really green, unripened papaya. This will get you the desired color, which is a light grayish-yellowish hue.

You can also use a slightly more ripened papaya, whose flesh is a light orange/pink color and texture a bit more tender. Cook the same and but add ½ cup (100 g) less sugar. The taste will be a bit different, naturally, but really good still. Using two different colors makes for really pretty plating and serving.

GLOSSARY

ACHIOTE OR ANNATTO. These two are used interchangeably and are the most common names for a commercial product extracted from the seeds of the evergreen *Bixa orellana* shrub/tree. Soak in warm water to extract the color. This is a great substitute for saffron. See page 29 for an oil-based alternative.

BROTH. The liquid produced from cooking meats or vegetables, or a combination of the two, in water. It is then used to cook food. Also known as bouillon.

BROWN. To cook food (usually meat) over high heat briefly until the surface turns brown without cooking through the interior. This adds a rich flavor to the food. This can be done in the pressure cooker if it is the first step in a recipe.

DEMILUNE. A U- or half-moon-shaped cut, typically referring to vegetables.

FLANERA. A metal mold shaped and specifically used to make flan or other custards.

JULIENNE. To cut vegetables, fruits or cheeses into thin strips.

MARINATE. The soaking process of food in a seasoned, often acidic, liquid before cooking. When time permits, allow a meat to marinate in the refrigerator.

MOJO. A liquid marinade, usually made with citrus fruits and a good amount of dried herbs and spices. Mostly used to season meats. Can also refer to a combination of dry and wet ingredients cooked together to season and flavor cooked foods.

PRESSURE REGULATOR. A valve that automatically cuts off the flow of a liquid or gas at a certain pressure level.

PRESSURE. The force applied perpendicular to the surface of an object per unit area over which that force is distributed.

PSI. Pounds per square inch (2.5 cm) above the existing atmospheric pressure. Water in a pressure cooker can reach a temperature of up to 250°F (120°C), depending on altitude.

RENDER. To melt animal fat over low heat until it turns brown and crispy. The result is a clear fat that is strained using a sieve or cheesecloth.

SAFFRON. Used to color food. A dried yellow stigma from a small purple crocus. Each flower provides only three stigmas, which must be carefully hand-picked and then dried, an extremely labor-intensive process. It takes 225,000 stigmas to make one pound (455 g) of saffron, making it the most expensive spice in the world. Use it sparingly in rice and certain meat dishes to give them color and taste.

SAUTÉ. To cook food in little fat and over high heat. The word comes from the French verb *sautér*, which means "to jump," and describes not only how food reacts when placed in a hot pan but also the method of tossing the food in the pan. Times vary depending on the amount of food and on the pan and the recipe the food is going into.

SHAVE. To cut wide, paper-thin slices of food, especially Parmesan cheese, vegetables or chocolate. Shave off slices with a vegetable peeler and use as garnish.

STOCK. The remaining liquid from cooking bones and connective tissues from meat proteins, in water. Then used to cook food. Stocks have more flavor impact than do broths.

SWEAT. The process of cooking onions in light fat (oil or butter) over low heat, stirring constantly to evaporate any water that may escape otherwise. Sweating usually results in tender, sometimes translucent, pieces.

TRUFFLE. A tuber fungus (mushroom) that grows underground at the root of a variety of trees, including beech, poplar, oak and others. Highly fragrant and expensive, it's regarded as somewhat elusive and used in fine cuisine. Gourmet, fine food shops and some grocery store chains, such as Whole Foods and Wegmans, typically sell truffles in season, most commonly the black winter Périgord truffle. At the time of publishing, the going price for black truffles was $1,570 per pound (455 g). White truffles, native to Alba, Italy, are significantly more expensive and hence harder to find in the United States.

ACKNOWLEDGMENTS

Life has a funny way of meandering its own uncharted journey. I owe this book to many, but these below have contributed to the heartbeat of a career you couldn't have paid me to believe I'd create.

Everyone close to me knows I'm in love with my mother. It's an obsession with a human being who epitomizes everything you aspire to be: mother, wife, friend, prayer warrior and relentlessly selfless caregiver to the stranger in need; all with a spectacular set of gifted hands to cook food that changes peoples' lives. If you've broken bread at my parents' house, you know this. This book is for you, *mi bella* Mami. I would not have found courage or joy in writing this book but not for your fervent support, tireless days and nights spent together in the kitchen and those constant singing voicemails. Next to God, you are my strength and reason for breathing. This is as much your book as it is mine. Thank you for allowing me to be your sweet honeydew and for letting me be authentically me when I insisted on learning how to cook. To my dad, for nurturing my passion for art in various forms and teaching me at 6 years old how to slice sweet plantains.

My blood squad, George, Karen, Jonathan and Christopher; thanks for being my best friends. For being so timely with all of your group text messages during the cooking and writing process. Also, for pitting me against Mami's food—because that challenged me to do better. Sister—especially you—for loving my applesauce as much as you do and for being the first one to pre-order this book. I really hope each of you buys a pressure cooker and makes these recipes. I love you so much.

My first-ever editor, Nick Chiles . . . Brother, do you know the journey you helped me pave many years ago when I was an eager travel writer exploring food? Thank you for critiquing my work and sincerely enjoying my writing—not an easily dished compliment from a *New York Times* and Pulitzer Prize–winning and bestselling, Harvard grad author. Thank you for giving me an opportunity.

My attorney and friend Drew is wildly talented beyond formal legalese and, with his reeducation of my legal studies, saved me a lot of money. Sean Johnson of Jo Blo Entertainment has dedicated his spare time to reignite the drive behind my passion for creating meaningful work. Leon Smith—probably my most loyal teddy bear who will always answer my call no matter my need.

To my girlfriends Simone, Taj and Farah. You already know, *chicas*. You have become the family I chose. Moni, thank you for giving it to me straight and just understanding my crazy over the last decade. I'm honored to call you sister. Barry, thank you for introducing me to American soul food 20+ years ago, especially those collard greens!

To my friend, Keith. Few words can express my gratitude for your presence while I cooked my way into the manuscript. The all-nighters, the grocery runs, the cards and the journeys. Thank you for your friendship over the past 17 years.

I could not have assumed the accuracy of all of the recipes without my testers Vivian, Christina, Vanessa, Maria, my cousins Dawn and Serena, and especially Joi (who bought two pressure cookers just for this). Thank you, ladies, for being so brave and pressure cooking for the first time with draft recipes. Your time and honest feedback was a vital piece of what's in this book. To chef and friend, Ronaldo Linares, for taking time out of his

(continued)

ACKNOWLEDGMENTS (CONT.)

restaurant to help me refine some recipes and offering his classically trained expertise. Tiffany, thank you for the research I needed done and indulging my passion for bringing pressure cooking to our generation and beyond. Marisela, *gracias por prestarme tu tiempo y haber mantenido mi cocina, y manera de atender mis detallitos.*

To my friend, longtime graphic designer and photographer, Dave Patterson, for never turning me down when I needed everything and anything. You generously took an unusual amount to time to bring my vision to life in a way only you could. Thank you from the bottom of my heart.

To the readers of Flanboyant Eats, social media friends and followers, clients and colleagues. Your support of my blog since 2008 led me here today. Thank you for following this journey and allowing me to inspire you. Thanks to all of the outlets, both print and online, that exposed my Cuban roots and the intimate role food has played in everything I've done, specifically NPR and Elayne Fluker, my former editor who offered me my first weekly food column.

My dear friend and mentor Lissette is a beautiful spirit whose meticulous work as an Emmy-winning TV producer found and granted me the most unrestricted platform to cook and talk about my love of food. Rainy, Alicia, Chemene and Vivian . . . the ladies of Studio 1A. I'm immensely humbled by your trust in my work and lending your audience to grow my platform. I know with certainty the sum of seven minutes invited this book. We are going to party, eat and toast after I teach Tamron how to use a pressure cooker!

My niece Priscilla displayed dedication during and after the photo shoot for this book, which rendered me delirious. Girl, those 6 a.m. FaceTimes to show me the fresh herb options were epic!

To the amazing team that is Ken Goodman and Bianca Borges. How did I get so remarkably lucky to have two chefs, New York–based industry veterans and rock-star food connoisseurs to act as my stylist and photographer for this book? Ken, thanks for the music and sharing the uncanny synergy we have. Bianca, my friend, thank you for epitomizing professionalism from the time we spoke for my first *Today* appearance. You've become my culinary mentor. Thank you for believing in my work and being my student in the magic of pressure-cooking. Sam Brown, thank you for stepping in at a wild moment and helping me create more magic with your defining eye. Your grace is lovely and the cover is everything I wanted. Thank you, thank you!

Finally, to the entire team at Page Street Publishing that worked relentlessly to bring forth this book. Will, I'm not sure I can properly articulate how humbled I am you asked me to pen the book I've been dreaming of for over a decade. For blindly trusting and believing I am the perfect person to reinvigorate the art of pressure cooking. Sarah, for your patience and understanding when I was overbooked with work and for trying to help me meet deadlines. Thank you all for the permissive nature of this process in giving me the blank canvas to share my food story.

My Atlanta family (you know who you are)—thank you. I'd be remiss if I didn't thank Chef Joël Robuchon and his team, specifically Odile Guinon (R.I.P.) and Phillip Braun, for giving me five unforgettable hours in your Manhattan atelier, where my understanding of the art and superb craftsmanship of cooking and being diligent about the integrity of a single ingredient was seeded. Green dots have never been so sexy. *Merci por tous les sentiments aimables que vous avez exprimé sur ma crème caramel. J'espère de vous regaler a nouveau.*

This book is a true testament that dreams do come true. You simply have to dream.

Peace, love and sexy food, B—

ABOUT THE AUTHOR

Bren is a Cuban-American, award-winning private chef, food and travel writer and lifestyle expert. She's been featured on the *Today* show, CNN, CBS, ABC, FOX, Telemundo and a host of print and online outlets including Saveur's Top Blogs, *Huffington Post*, *Glamour* magazine and the *Washington Post*, to name a few. She's currently working as a recipe developer and TV spokesperson for several household-name brands. She lives in Washington, D.C., with her faithful Cavachon, Paris Prince. Learn more at BrenHerrera.com, where she curates her passion for food, cooking, traveling and her Afro-Latin roots.

INDEX